Finders & Keepers of Faith

a puzzling approach

MJ Caimbeul

First published by Busybird Publishing 2019
Copyright © 2019 M. J. Caimbeul

ISBN 978-0-6484789-9-7

Cover image: Kev Howlett, Busybird Publishing
Cover design: Busybird Publishing
Layout and typesetting: Busybird Publishing
Editor: Laura McCluskey

busybird
publishing

Busybird Publishing
2/118 Para Road
Montmorency, Victoria
Australia 3094
www.busybird.com.au

Contents

How to Use This Booklet

This publication is intended to identify key areas of faith and scripture. It presents a variety of activities and vignettes to engage interest and involvement as well as to provoke thought.

Most puzzles are accompanied by answers overleaf. Some users may find it helpful to study the answer sheets first and then, after a suitable time lapse, test their grasp of content with the puzzle itself. This strategy is useful with classes.

Puzzles could prove useful projects with topics for research pre-advised.

Ready access to reference material is recommended.

Puzzles may be chosen randomly or to fit in with a theme.

Some users might care to include selected activities to enrich festive occasions such that the real meaning of the celebration is foremost. This will prove to be a bonding and fun experience for the group. The materialistic aspect of the day is thus diminished.

Note that there are many versions of the Bible, each with its nuances of language and layout. Anticipate some of these subtle distinctions.

Prepare to meet many interesting characters on your journey from cover to cover.

Foreword

Several versions of the Bible were consulted in the writing of this booklet. Hence, variations in the spelling of names and places as well as slight differences in line references may be apparent.

It is dedicated to the values that have sustained and protected civilised societies, values which are the keystone of stability:

Charity	*Compassion*	*Courage*
Faith	*Fairness*	*Fidelity*	*Friendship*
Honesty	*Honour*	*Love*	*Just Law*
Hope	*Reason*	*Respect*	*Selflessness*
Stoicism	*Tolerance*	*Trustworthiness*

I found these in some of the wonderful people recorded in books of the Bible.

This booklet is for you, your family, your friends, your class, your students and anyone wishing to enjoy exploring Bible narratives.

You may also find it a practical and enjoyable way to shift the focus from materialism to the real reason we celebrate some festive occasions.

"Do not worry about tomorrow.
Tomorrow will take care of itself.
Each day has enough trouble of its own."
Matthew 6:34

About Time!

The measurement of time is man's invention.

There was no universally accepted calendar until the 20th century, the Gregorian calendar being now currently used. Pope Gregory XIII initiated this calendar in 1582. It was then used by those with allegiance to Rome. Great Britain and her American colonies (as they were then called) came on board in 1751. Russia, Greece and the Balkans followed in the early 20th century. This replaced the Julian calendar introduced in 46 BC and so it was by now 10 days behind. Thus dates had to jump forward by that interval, the 4th October being followed by the 15th October. Britain did a 'fast-forward' in 1751. Up until then, their year had always started on 25th March and finished at the end of February, not December. To adjust, in 1751, from 1st January till 24th March (which fell at the end of year) was dropped off so that the 1752 year could commence on 1st January, 1752 (not 25th March). So, sorting out Time has not been easy! *What then in Biblical times?*

Measuring time with some consistency requires use of a reliable standard unit. The more consistent units were the 'natural' units, that is, units derived from occurrences (or recurrences) in nature e.g.

- a solar day (high noon to next high noon, using the shortest shadow cast by the sun);
- a month (1 orbit of the moon around the earth, or 1 new moon till the next);
- a year (1 complete orbit of earth around sun, or from 1 spring / autumn equinox till the next of the same kind)

Thus a week and an hour are not natural units. *So, who used what?*

The Babylonians devised a calendar in the 4th millennium BC. It had 24 'hours' per day.

The Chinese had a 12 'hour' day and the Hindus had a 60 'hour' day. The Sumerians had 360 days in a year of 12 months. *At some time*, the Hebrews set a week at 7 days (of Creation) with 52 weeks thus 364 days per year (Dead Sea Scroll sect). This eventually leads to seasons being 'out of step' with the calendar, or seeming to fall into an uncharacteristic pattern weather-wise.

How might they interpret this? What time scales were employed in their early recorded history, or in that of others around them?

Jesus was born when the Roman empire used the Julian calendar. The Gospel of Luke (3:1 & 3:23) gives Jesus' age as *approximately* 30 years coinciding with the 15th year of rule of Tiberias Caesar who became emperor from 14 AD. Adding the numbers seems to suggest a birth in 1 AD (Anno Domini – in the year of our Lord). But – the age cited is only approximate and may not at that time have been considered important. The disciple, Matthew, recounts details of the birth during the reign of Herod the Great who died in 4 BC. Following the birth, Joseph, Mary and Jesus had sought safety in Egyptian lands and did not return until after Herod's death. Suggestions of a birth year of 5 / 6 / 7 BC do not seem unreasonable.

Try drawing a timeline of Jesus' life marking birth, start of his ministry, death . . .

(NB: The Romans did not use zero so 1BC precedes 1AD. Thus a timeline ≠ a mathematical number line.)

⟶

Suggestion: To calculate ages or times, start at left and count the number of intervals/years.
For example, from 5BC to 5AD would be 9 years.

1

What is time? (Room for your thoughts!)

- ❖ A sequence of happenings
  what has happened; what is happening now; what lies ahead
- ❖ ....
- ❖ ....

What is a year?

- ❖ The time taken for the earth to orbit the sun
- ❖ The time taken for the sun to return to the apparent position at which it started or was observed to be
- ❖ The time reckoned by the sun changing its apparent position from overhead at the Tropic of Capricorn (latitude 23^0 27^1 S) to overhead at the Tropic of Cancer (latitude 23^0 27^1 N) AND its return
  This is the inter-tropical year or the tropical year (between the Tropics) and is also reckoned as the time between successive vernal / spring equinoxes.
- ❖ The length of the four seasons caused by the changing position of the sun (*spring, summer, autumn, winter*)
- ❖ The cycle of named months and days (of 24 hours) from the start of one calendar year to the next. *This is known as a civil year.* It needs to be the same length as the tropical year so a periodic adjustment to the civil calendar of 1 day every 4 years is required.
- ❖ The time reckoned for the sun to return to an observed position in relation to 'fixed' stars. *This is known as a sidereal year.* Its length differs from that of a tropical year.
- ❖ ....

Consider the contributions of Julius Caesar, Dionysius Exiguus, Pope Gregory XIII and John Harrison to recording of time. (You may find others of interest.)

When time stood still

(Joshua 10: 12,13) *And he said in the sight of Israel, 'Sun, stand still over Gibeon, and, moon, you also, over the Vale of Aijalon'. And the sun stood still, and the moon halted . . .* (about a day)

(2 Kings 20: 8-11) *Hezekiah said to Isaiah, 'What is the sign to tell me that Yahweh will cure me and that I shall be going up to the Temple of Yahweh in three days?' 'Here' Isaiah replied 'is the sign from Yahweh that He will do what He has said. Would you like the shadow to go forward 10 steps, or go back 10 steps?' 'It is easy for the shadow to lengthen 10 steps,' Hezekiah answered. 'No, I would rather the shadow went back 10 steps.' The prophet Isaiah then called on Yahweh who made the shadow go back 10 steps on the steps of Ahaz.*

So, have we here on earth lost some time?

The Book of Joshua says 'about a day' or, 23 hours 20 minutes in today's reckoning. That is, 'about' a day. The Book of Kings refers to 10 steps lost, perhaps 10 degrees or 40 minutes.

That would combine to a whole day.

If a day ceased to, quite literally, exist, what else would be affected – then, now and in the future?

....

J
E
S
U
S

Mark 12:11
It was the stone rejected by the builders that became the keystone.
This was the Lord's doing and it is wonderful to see.

Isaiah 11
A shoot will come up from the stump of Jesse;
from his roots a branch will bear fruit.
The spirit of the Lord will rest on him –
the Spirit of wisdom and of understanding,
The Spirit of counsel and of power,
the Spirit of knowledge and of the fear of the Lord –
and he will delight in the fear of the Lord.

He will not judge by what he sees with his eyes, or decide by what he hears with his ears; but with righteousness he will judge the needy,
with justice he will give decisions for the poor of the earth.

He will strike the earth with the rod of his mouth;
with the breath of his lips he will slay the wicked.

Righteousness will be his belt and faithfulness the sash around his waist. . . . .

Mark 13:24
'The coming of the Son of Man'
But in those days, after that time of distress, the sun will be darkened, the moon will lose its brightness, the stars will come falling from heaven and the powers in the heavens will be shaken.

And then they will see the Son of Man coming in the clouds with great power and glory; then too he will send the angels to gather his chosen from the four winds, from the ends of the world to the ends of heaven.

Jeremiah
And they took the thirty silver pieces, the sum at which the precious one was priced by children of Israel, and they gave them for the potter's field, just as the Lord directed me.

☆ ★ ☆ ★ ☆ ★ ☆ ★ ☆

'There are many rooms in my Father's house; if there were not, I should have told you.'

'Love your neighbor as yourself.'

'Blessed are the poor in spirit,
for theirs is the kingdom of heaven.
Blessed are those who mourn,
for they will be comforted.
Blessed are the meek,
for they will inherit the earth.
Blessed are those who hunger and thirst for righteousness,
for they will be satisfied.
Blessed are the merciful,
for they will be shown mercy.
Blessed are the pure in heart,
For they will see God.
Blessed are the peacemakers,
For they will be called sons of God.
Blessed are those who are persecuted in the cause of right,
for theirs is the kingdom of heaven.'

'Our Father in heaven
may your name be held holy,
your kingdom come,
your will be done
on earth as in heaven.
Give us today our daily bread.
And forgive us our debts
As we have forgiven those
who are in debt to us.
And do not put us to the test,
but deliver us from the evil one.'
Matthew 6:9 (Jerusalem bible version)

GENEALOGY OF JESUS CHRIST

Matthew 1:1 *(Stepfather, Joseph's line)*		Genesis; Ruth; *1Chronicles: 1–3 and Luke 3:23-38*	Luke 3:23-38 *(continued)*
Abraham (Generation)	1	Adam	Nathan
Isaac	2	Seth	Mattatha
Jacob	3	Enosh	Menna
Judah	4	Kenan /	Melea
Perez	5	Cainan	Eliakim
Hezron	6	Mahalalel	Jonam
Ram	7	Jared	Joseph
Amminadab	8	Enoch	Judah
Nahshon	9	Methusaleh	Symeon
Salmon	10	Lamech	Levi
Boaz	11	Noah	Matthat
Obed	12	Shem	Jorim
Jesse	13	Arpachshad /	Eliezer
King David	**14**	Arphaxad	Joshua
Solomon	1	Cainan (*Luke*)	Er
Rehoboam	2	Shelah	Elmadam
Abijah	3	Eber	Cosam
Asa	4	Peleg	Addi
Jeoshaphat	5	Reu	Melchi
Joram/Jehoram	6	Serug	Neri
Azariah/Uzziah	7	Nahor	Shealtiel
Jotham	8	Terah	Zerubbabel
Ahaz	9	Abram / Abraham	Rhesa
Hezekiah	10		Joanan
Manasseh	11	*Luke 3:23-38 continues*	Joda
Amon	12	*genealogy of Mary,*	Josech
Josiah	13	*mother of Jesus*	Semein
Jechoniah *to* Babylon	**14**		Mattathias
Jechoniah *after* Babylon	1	1. *from Abraham*	Maath
Shealtiel	2	2. Isaac	Naggai
Zerubbabel	3	3. Jacob	Esli
Abiud	4	4. Judah	Nahum
Eliakim	5	5. Perez	Amos
Azor	6	6. Hezron	Mattathias
Zadok	7	7. Ram / Arni	Joseph
Achim	8	8. Amminadab	Jannai
Eliud	9	9. Nahshon	Melchi
Eleazar	10	10. Salmon / Sala /	Levi
Matthan	11	Salma	Matthat
Jacob/Israel	12	11. Boaz	Heli (father of Mary)
Joseph–		12. Obed	Joseph (Heli's
(Betrothed of Mary)	13	13. Jesse	son-in-law) &
Jesus called Christ	**14**	**14. King David** *then*	Mary, mother of Jesus
			Jesus called Christ

'Why speak in parables?' Matt. 13:14

'It is given unto you (the disciples) to know the mysteries of the Kingdom of Heaven, but to them (the multitudes) it is not given.'

Jesus shared His wisdom through the speaking in parables. Each parable told thus teaches an important lesson both in faith and its practice. Select one of these parables. Read it then share the story together with the message woven into its words. Do this with your class, family or friends, orally or written.

1. **PARABLE OF THE SOWER**
   (Sermon on the seashore)   Matt. 13:3; Mark 4:3; Luke 8:5

2. **THE LABOURERS IN THE VINEYARD**
   (Teaching the self-righteous)   Matt. 20:1

3. **THE UNMERCIFUL SERVANT**
   (Answering Peter – *How oft shall I forgive?*)   Matt. 18:23

4. **THE TWO SONS**
   (The chief priests demand his authority)   Matt. 21:28

5. **THE TEN VIRGINS**
   (Prophesying the Second Advent)   Matt. 25:1

6. **THE GOOD SAMARITAN**
   (The lawyer's question: *Who is my neighbour?)*   Luke 10:25

7. **THE LOST SHEEP**
   (Response to 'murmuring' of Pharisees & scribes)   Luke 15:4; Matt.18:12

8. **THE PRODIGAL SON**
   ((Response to 'murmuring' of Pharisees & scribes)   Luke 15:11

9. **THE GREAT SUPPER**
   (In answer to one dining with Him)   Luke 14:16

10. **THE WHEAT AND THE TARES**
    (Sermon on the seashore)   Matt. 13:24

Step Back in Time ~ 2000 years !

The disciples walked amongst and preached to organised communities.
People were employed in many varied occupations. The Bible provides abundant clues.
Consider occupations that would have been possible in each of the nominated areas below.
Compare and discuss what you have listed in each.   What was your evidence?

Entertainment:-	**Defence:-**
Government & Public Service:-	**Finance:-**
Infrastructure:-	**Clothing & Adornment:-**

Construction:-	Home & Contents:-
Food & Beverages:-	Transport, Travel & Tourism:-
Mining:-	Education & Religion:-

MAKING MIGHTY MEMORIES

Train your mind to remember up to 21 randomly chosen things. This can be a fun exercise.

To prepare yourself (by yourself), write numbers 1 to 21 on a sheet of paper. Beside each number, write the name of something you can easily associate with that number. A name with a picture will help you to remember. A list has been done for you. Memorise your word or phrase with each number. Rhymes can make it easier to recall the association. *You could use 'The 12 Days of Christmas'.*

1. **One son**	12. **Disciples**
2. **A shoe**	13. **Curtain**
3. **Free**	14. **Fortnight**
4. **At the door**	15. **<u>Drift</u>-ing**
5. **A live beehive**	16. **Sweet 16**
6. **Bricks**	17. **Driver's licence**
7. **Colours of the rainbow**	18. **Vote**
8. **The Pearly Gate**	19. **Pine tree**
9. **In a line**	20. **All fingers and toes**
10. **Commandments**	21. **Key to the door**
11. **In heaven**	

Practise reciting numbers and associated words until the links become 'second nature'. You should be able to say them forwards, backwards and randomly. **Do this part by yourself.**

THEN

In a group, invite members to write numbers 1 to 21 on a chart or board. Let them suggest any random thing to be written beside each number. Tell them you can remember 21 items in 5 minutes. Now mentally link each word on the chart to the words embedded in your memorised list. The link you make can be ridiculous just as long as you make an association e.g. if 'hat' was written beside 1, you might think 'one son wearing hat' (using the 'one' in the box above). And e.g. if 'cake' was written beside 20, using the link in the box above, you might think 'fingers and toes dug into the cake'. Only you know what mental link you are making. The group does not know you have a mental template. Try to form a mind picture to match your words. Importantly, none of the group has any idea what you are thinking. *Practice will speed up this process!*

Turn away from the chart / board. Invite the group to call any number and you can confidently tell them what was written beside that number. For fun, name the odd or even objects, backwards or forwards. *You must be a genius!!!!*

'Job Search'

Applying for a job? Step back in time 2000 years. 18 jobs that people did are hidden in the grid – horizontally, vertically, backwards or forwards. Some were hereditary, compulsory or unpaid, but mostly, it was work or starve! Mark each one you find and enter it below.

C	O	U	N	S	E	L	L	O	R	S
A	C	T	O	R	S	E	E	R	O	W
R	E	M	R	A	F	Z	S	E	T	I
P	R	I	E	S	T	W	E	L	I	N
E	E	N	M	I	N	E	R	L	C	E
N	T	S	A	N	O	A	V	E	I	H
T	T	T	G	G	S	V	A	W	L	E
E	O	R	I	E	A	E	N	E	O	R
R	P	E	X	R	M	R	T	J	S	D
S	I	L	V	E	R	S	M	I	T	H

1.	7.	13.
2.	8.	14.
3.	9.	15.
4.	10.	16.
5.	11.	17.
6.	12.	18.

Score . . . / 18   The 2 letters left are ___ and ___.   (Answers overleaf)

Answers to 'Job Search'

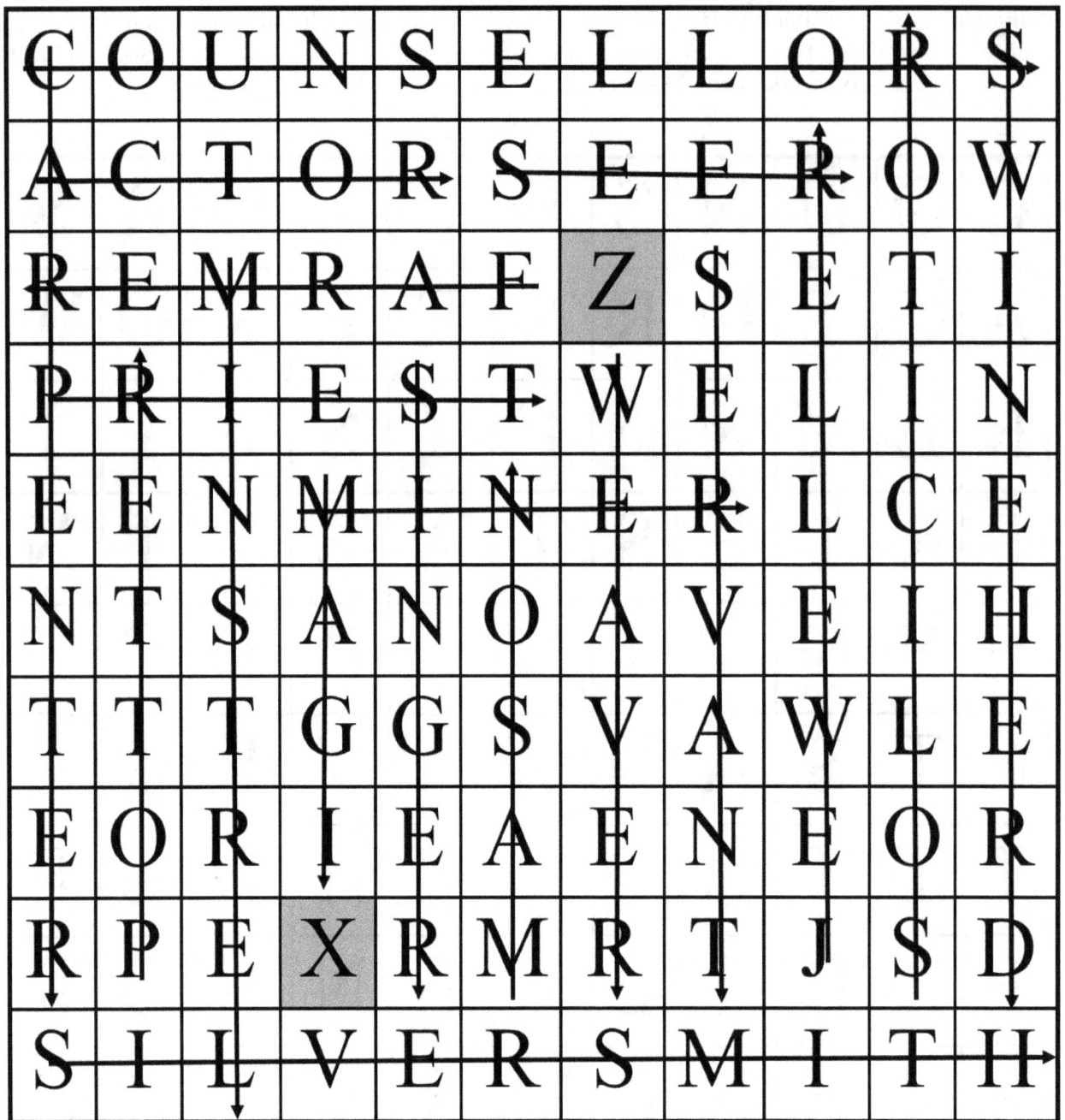

C	O	U	N	S	E	L	L	O	R	S
A	C	T	O	R	S	E	E	R	O	W
R	E	M	R	A	F	Z	S	E	T	I
P	R	I	E	S	T	W	E	L	I	N
E	E	N	M	I	N	E	R	L	C	E
N	T	S	A	N	O	A	V	E	I	H
T	T	T	G	G	S	V	A	W	L	E
E	O	R	I	E	A	E	N	E	O	R
R	P	E	X	R	M	R	T	J	S	D
S	I	L	V	E	R	S	M	I	T	H

1. Counsellors
2. Actor
3. Seer
4. Farmer
5. Priest
6. Miner
7. Silversmith
8. Carpeneter(s)
9. Potter
10. Minstrel
11. Magi
12. Singer
13. Mason
14. Weaver(s)
15. Servant
16. Jeweller
17. Solicitor
18. Swineherd

Answers 1 to 7 are horizontal; 8 to 18 vertical.   The letters left over are Z and X.

Getting things in order

Can you place these in chronological order? Use numbers to indicate your decision. (1= earliest)

A. Books of the New Testament: John ___ ; Mark ___ ; Matthew ___ ; The Acts ___ ; Luke ___

B. People of the Old Testament: Methusaleh ___ ; Adam ___ ; Enoch ___ ; Seth ___ ; Cainan ___ ; Noah _____

C. Events in the Book of Genesis: The Great Flood ___ ; God's call to Abraham ___ ; Temptation by the serpent in the garden ___ ; The Tower of Babel ___ ; Birth of Ishmael ___

D. (1 Corinthians 15)

   Succession of witnesses to the Resurrection of Christ: Saul of Tarsus ___ ; some 500 brethren together ___ ; Cephas then the 11 disciples ___ ; all the apostles ___

E. Events prior to the death of Jesus: The governor's soldiers made a crown of thorns ___ ; Pilate washes his hands ___ ; Simon from Cyrene carries the cross ___ ; Jesus is scourged ___

F. Events at Golgotha (Place of the skull): Jesus' side pierced with a lance ___ ; soldiers offer Jesus wine mixed with gall ___ ; darkness falls for 3 hours ___ ; soldiers cast lots for his clothing ___ ; "Father, into your hands I commit my spirit" ___

G. Some of the plagues of Egypt: death of 1st born ___ ; locusts ___ ; blood ___ ; hail ___

H. 'Days' of Creation: Let the water teem with living creatures ___ ; Let dry land appear and the earth produce vegetation ___ ; Let there be light ___ ; God blesses the 7th day ___ ; Let there be a vault in the waters – heaven and earth ___ ; Let there be lights in the vault (heaven) ___ ; Let the earth produce living creatures and let us make man in our image ___

I. Historical events of the Hebrews: Temple of Solomon started ___ ; Romans rule the Holy Lands ___ ; 10 Commandments received ___ ; 430 years slavery in Egypt ___ ; 70 years captivity in Babylon ___

Score 1 for each correct entry. My score is _____.
(45 possible answers. Difficult!   Answers overleaf.)

Getting things in order

A. Matthew **1**; Mark **2**; Luke **3**; John **4**; The Acts **5**

B. Adam **1**; Seth **2**; Cainan **3**; Enoch **4**; Methusaleh **5**; Noah **6**

C. Temptation by serpent **1**; The Great Flood **2**; The Tower of Babel **3**; God's call to Abraham **4**; Birth of Ishmael **5**

D. (1 Corinthians 15)
Cephas then the 11 disciples **1**; some 500 brethren together **2**; all the apostles **3**; Saul of Tarsus **4**

E. Pilate washes his hands **1**; Jesus is scourged **2**; Soldiers made a crown of thorns **3**; Simon from Cyrene carries cross **4**

F. soldiers offer Jesus wine with gall **1**; soldiers cast lots for his clothing **2**; darkness falls for 3 hours **3**; "Father, into your hands I commit my spirit" **4**; Jesus' side pierced with a lance **5**

G. blood **1**; hail **2**; locusts **3**; death of 1st born **4**

H. Let there be light **1**; Let there be a <u>vault</u> in the waters – <u>heaven,</u> earth **2**; Let dry land appear and the earth produce vegetation **3**; Let there be lights in heaven **4**; Let the water teem with living creatures **5**; Let the earth produce living creatures and let us make man in our image **6**; God blesses the 7th day **7**

I. 430 years slavery in Egypt **1**; 10 Commandments received **2**; Temple of Solomon started **3**; 70 years captivity in Babylon **4**; Romans rule the Holy Lands **5**

Set in Stone: *The Decalogue*

I am the Lord your God, who brought you out of Egypt, out of the land of slavery. You shall have no other Gods before me.

You shall not make for yourself an idol in the form of anything in heaven above or on the earth beneath or in the waters below. You shall not bow down to them or worship them; for I, the Lord your God, am a jealous God, punishing the children for the sin of the fathers to the third and fourth generation of those who hate me, but showing love to thousands of those who love me and keep my commandments.

You shall not misuse the name of the Lord your God for the Lord will not hold anyone guiltless who misuses his name.

Observe the Sabbath day by keeping it holy, as the Lord your God has commanded you. Six days you shall labour and do all your work, but the seventh day is a Sabbath to the Lord your God. On it you shall not do any work neither you, nor your son or daughter, nor your manservant nor maidservant, nor your ox, your donkey or any of your animals, nor the stranger within your gates, so that your manservant and maidservant may rest as you do. Remember that you were slaves in Egypt and that the Lord your God brought you out of there with a mighty hand and an outstretched arm: therefore the Lord your God commands you to observe the Sabbath day.

Honour your father and your mother, as the Lord your God has commanded you, so that you may live long and that it may go well with you in the land the Lord your God is giving you.

You shall not murder.

You shall not commit adultery.

You shall not steal.

Neither shall you bear false witness against your neighbour.

You shall not covet your neighbour's wife, nor shall you desire your neighbour's house or land, his manservant or his maidservant, his ox or donkey, or anything else that belongs to your neighbour.

TIMELINE – What happened when?

Place the events below in chronological order close to the year when each may have occurred.		
	Approx 4000 B.C.	
	B.C. OR B.C.E.	
	Approx 3000 B.C. (3200)	
Herod, King of Jews	~2400 B.C.	
Lazarus raised from dead		
	~1700 B.C.	
Temple of Solomon commenced	~1650 B.C.	
John the Baptist baptises Jesus	Approx 1270 B.C.	
The Last Supper	1250 B.C.	
Methuselah		
Prophet Isaiah lives	1050 B.C.	
Feast of Cana		
Lazarus raised from dead	966 B.C.	
The Deluge - Noah		
Feeding masses with loaves and fishes	700 B.C.	
Abraham and Sarah	Approx 350 B.C.	
Crucifixion and resurrection	Around 330 B.C.	Alexander the Great marches his armies
	63 B.C.	Pompey captures Judaea
Birth of Jesus	49 B.C.	Julius Caesar, Dictator of Rome
Daniel in lions' den	39 B.C.	
Jesus converts Saul of Tarsus (called Paul)		
	27 B.C.	Octavius / Augustus 1st Emperor of Rome
The Exodus from Egypt	Pre – 1AD	
Moses adopted by Pharaoh's daughter	1 A.D. / C.E.	
	Around 26 / 27 A.D.	
Joseph sold into slavery		
Jesus rides donkey into Jerusalem- Palm Sunday		
Time of Adam		
Time of King Saul then King David		
	30/33A.D.	

Some lines are blank! Some entries derive from oral tradition. Others are historically confirmed.
Answers overleaf.

ANSWERS TO

TIMELINE - What happened when?

Around 4000 B.C. / B.C.E. estimated by some bible scholars	Time of Adam
Around 3000 B.C. (3200)	Methuselah (estimated from biblical sequence)
2400 B.C.	The Deluge / Great Flood: Noah
1700 B.C.	Abraham & Sarah
1650 B.C.	Joseph sold into slavery
Around 1270 B.C.	Moses adopted by Pharaoh's daughter
1250 B.C.	The Exodus from Egypt
1050 B.C.	Time of King Saul then King David
966 B.C.	Temple of Solomon commenced
700 B.C.	Isaiah the Prophet lives
Around 350 B.C.	Daniel in the lions' den (Babylon)
330 B.C.	Alexander the Great marches his armies
63 B.C.	Pompey captures Judaea
49 B.C.	Julius Caesar, Dictator of Rome
39 B.C.	Herod the Great, King of the Jews
27 B.C.	Octavius/Augustus, 1st Roman Emperor
Some years later	Birth of Jesus
1 A.D. or C.E.	
Around 26/27 A.D./C.E.	John the Baptist baptises Jesus
	Feast of Cana – turning water to wine
	Feeding masses with fishes and loaves
	Lazarus raised from dead
	Jesus rides donkey into Jerusalem
	The Last Supper
30/33 A.D.	Crucifixion, Resurrection
	Jesus converts Saul of Tarsus (became Paul)

11 Faithful Apostles	# The Apostle # Andrew
Peter	❖ Brother of Peter / Simon Peter
John - The Evangelist	
& James, His Brother	❖ Jewish fisherman
Andrew	❖ Of Galilee
Philip	❖ Follower of John the Baptist
Thomas	
Bartholomew	❖ First of the Apostles to follow Jesus
Matthew	❖ Preached the Good News to the Greeks
James – Son of	❖ Was martyred by crucifixion in 60 A.D.
Alphaeus	
Simon The Zealot	❖ Andrew's relics reside in Patras, Greece
Jude – Son of James (*Thaddaeus*)	

The apostles were witnesses to the words and works of Jesus (Jeshua).

They recorded what they had seen and heard in their gospels.

The Apostle
Peter

Named 'Peter' by Jesus. His name was 'Simon'. Peter derives from the Greek word *petros* meaning *rock* or *stone*, hence called (Simon) Peter, the rock on which to build His church. Jesus was made known to Simon (Peter) by his brother Andrew.

❖ Born in Bethsaida of Galilee

❖ Successful Jewish fisherman & boat owner

❖ With brother, Andrew, fished with James and John (sons of Zebedee)

❖ Commissioned by Christ to preach the Good News to Jews of the Diaspora

❖ Travelled widely . . . Antioch . . . Rome

❖ Persecuted and imprisoned for his mission

❖ Martyred (believed to have been crucified upside down during Nero's purges in Rome)

In 320 AD, the Roman Emperor Constantine the Great began construction of the basilica on the side of Vatican Hill over an enormous necropolis, likely Christian. Reports / Stories handed down over several generations compelled him to believe that the body of Peter had been laid to rest in this inhospitable place. Thus was the construction so positioned to honour the Apostle and Disciple, Simon Peter, interred below.

---

11 Faithful Apostles

Peter

John - The Evangelist

& James, His Brother

Andrew

Philip

Thomas

Bartholomew

Matthew

James – Son of

Alphaeus

Simon The Zealot

Jude – Son of James
(Thaddaeus)

Meet the workers!

Rearrange the letters to find out who might have crossed your path some 2000 years ago.

A '🌀' indicates a compound word e.g. goldsmith or 2 words naming an occupation.

(Solution overleaf.)

1. PINCERS	16. MURDER M!
2. DE JUG	17. NERD RAGE
3. CROAT	18. VALES
4. RED CAN	19. ACT PAIN
5. STRIPE	20. MAIN FRESH 🌀
6. COD ROT	21. JEER WELL
7. THE PROP	22. NET MARKET 🌀
8. OLD RISE	23. THICK BALMS 🌀
9. RIGNESS	24. SURER RATE
10. GINK	25. KRAW MEAL 🌀
11. FRAMER	26. NOTES ANSOM 🌀
12. WE RAVE!	27. CLAXETTOCROL 🌀
13. NET CHARM	28. BER BRIDE GUILD 🌀
14. IT SHARP	29. BITERM-GRETTE 🌀
15. INNER PEAK	30. WORD MAKERS 🌀

We are forgiven for our failures but not for failing to fight.

Meet the workers!

Solutions

1. PINCERS
   princes

2. DE JUG
   judge

3. CROAT
   actor

4. RED CAN
   dancer

5. STRIPE
   priest

6. COD ROT
   doctor

7. THE PROP
   prophet

8. OLD RISE
   soldier

9. RIGNESS
   singers

10. GINK
    king

11. FRAMER
    farmer

12. WE RAVE!
    weaver

13. NET CHARM
    merchant

14. IT SHARP
    harpist

15. INNER PEAK
    innkeeper

16. MURDER M!
    drummer

17. NERD RAGE
    gardener

18. VALES
    slave

19. ACT PAIN
    captain

20. MAIN FRESH ✿
    fisherman

21. JEER WELL
    jeweller

22. NET MARKET ✿
    tentmaker

23. THICK BALMS ✿
    blacksmith

24. SURER RATE
    treasurer

25. KRAW MEAL ✿
    lawmaker

26. NOTES ANSOM ✿
    stonemason

27. CLAXETTOCROL ✿
    tax-collector

28. BER BRIDE GUILD ✿
    bridge-builder

29. BITERM-GRETTE ✿
    timber-getter

30. WORD MAKERS ✿
    sword-maker

Those whom God touches,

however unlikely the choice may seem to us,

He imbues with zealous fire that cannot be extinguished,

just as certainly as He cannot be extinguished!

18

WHO SPOKE THESE WORDS?

Part 1

These words may sound familiar. Can you decide who is credited with uttering/writing them?

1. I am innocent of the blood of this just man. See ye to it._____

2. My father, behold the fire and the wood; but where is the lamb for a burnt offering? _____

3. We may eat of the fruit of the trees of the garden but of the fruit of the tree in the midst of the garden, God has said 'Ye shall not eat of it.' _____

4. Entreat me not to leave thee . . . for whither thou goest, I will go. _____

5. Bring me a sword . . . divide the living child in two and give half to one woman and half to the other. _____

6. The Lord is my shepherd; I shall not want. _____

7. It is better to dwell in the wilderness than with a contentious and an angry woman. _____

8. Behold, a virgin shall conceive and bear a son, and shall call his name Immanuel. _____

9. Death, where is your victory? Death, where is your sting? _____

10. Call the magicians and the astrologers and the sorcerers. (Which King?) _____

11. I have baptised with water but He shall baptise you with the Holy Spirit. _____

12. Hail, thou that art highly favoured, the Lord is with thee; blessed art thou among women. _____

13. Whomsoever I shall kiss, that same is He; take Him and lead Him away safely. _____

14. Every son that is born ye shall cast into the river and every daughter ye shall save alive. _____

15. What shall I ask for? The head of John the Baptist. _____

My score is . . . / 15

(Answers overleaf.)

WHO SPOKE THESE WORDS?

Answers for Part 1

Pontius Pilate Matthew 27:24	1. I am innocent of the blood of this just man
Isaac Genesis 22:7	2. My father, behold the fire and the wood but where is ...
Eve Genesis 3: 2-3	3. We may eat of the fruit of the trees of this garden but ...
Ruth Ruth 1:16	4. Entreat me not to leave thee .. for whither thou goest ...
Solomon 1Kings 3:24	5. Bring me a sword ... Divide the living child in two ...
David Psalm 23	6. The Lord is my shepherd; I shall not want ...
Solomon Proverbs 25:24	7. It is better to dwell in the wilderness ....
Isaiah Isaiah 7:14	8. Behold a virgin shall conceive and bear a son ...
Letter of Paul Corinthians 15:55	9. Death, where is your victory? Death, where is your sting?
Nebuchadnezzar Daniel 2:2,3	10. Call the magicians ...
John the Baptist Mark 1:8	11. I have baptised with water ...
The Angel, Gabriel Luke 1:28	12. Hail, thou that art highly favoured, the Lord is with thee ...
Judas Matthew 26:48	13. Whomsoever I kiss, that same is He ...
Pharaoh Exodus 1:22	14. Every son that is born ye shall cast into the river ...
Salome Matthew 14:8	15. What shall I ask for? The head of John the Baptist. *The name Salome was recorded by the Jewish historian, Josephus, in the first century. Salome was the daughter of Herod and Herodias.*

PEOPLE & BOOKS OF
THE NEW TESTAMENT

There are 22 names of people and books of the New Testament in this grid. The names are horizontal (going either to right or to left) and vertical (going upwards or downwards).
Some letters are shared.
Draw a line through each one you discover and write its name in the space below.
12 letters not crossed make up a hidden message. What does it say? (Answers overleaf.)

C	A	I	A	P	H	A	S	J	R	Y
O	S	T	I	M	O	T	H	Y	E	R
L	A	R	E	T	E	P	E	S	V	A
O	L	O	N	U	M	S	M	I	E	M
S	I	M	O	N	A	P	A	U	L	H
S	S	A	M	L	T	N	R	S	A	E
I	S	N	I	U	T	H	K	A	T	B
A	E	S	T	A	H	O	R	M	I	R
N	D	S	U	S	E	J	I	O	O	E
S	U	T	I	T	W	S	E	H	N	W
N	J	A	M	E	S	A	C	T	S	S

Across: _____ _____ _____ _____

Down: _____ _____ _____ _____

_____ _____ _____ _____

_____ _____ _____ _____

1   2   3   4   5   6   7   8   9   10   11   12

____ ____ ____ ____ ____ ____ ____ ____ ____ ____ ____ ____

PEOPLE & BOOKS OF THE NEW TESTAMENT

C	A	I	A	P	H	A	S	J	R	Y
O	S	T	I	M	O	T	H	Y	E	R
L	A	R	E	T	E	P	E	S	V	A
O	L	O	N	U	M	S	M	I	E	M
S	I	M	O	N	A	P	A	U	L	H
S	S	A	M	L	T	N	R	S	A	E
I	S	N	I	U	T	H	K	A	T	B
A	E	S	T	A	H	O	R	M	I	R
N	D	S	U	S	E	J	I	O	O	E
S	U	T	I	T	W	S	E	H	N	W
N	J	A	M	E	S	A	C	T	S	S

Across: (Row number and direction: to right / to left)

1 Caiaphas rt	2 Timothy rt	3 Peter lt	5 Simon rt
5 Paul rt	9 Jesus lt	10 Titus lt	11 James rt	11 Acts rt

Down: (Column & Direction: up / down):

1 Colossians d	2 Silas u	2 Jude u	3 Romans d
4 Timon u;	5 Saul u	6 Matthew d;	7 John u;
8 Mark d	9 Thomas u	10 Revelations d	11 Mary u	11 Hebrews d

Hidden Message

1	2	3	4	5		6	7		8	9	10	11	12
J	E	S	U	S		I	S		R	I	S	E	N

Quick Quiz around the Christmas Tree

Work with a partner or by yourself.

Finish when most people have written their answers.

1. In which town was Jesus born? _ _ _ _ _ _ _ _ _ _ _ _

2. Who was the Roman Emperor who decreed that all the world at this time should be taxed (or be part of a census)? _ _ _ _ _ _ _ _ _ _ _ _ _ _ _ _ _ _ _

3. From which city in Galilee had the family travelled in accordance with the Emperor's decree? (They had to return to the place of their lineage.)
    _ _ _ _ _ _ _ _ _ _ _ _ _ _ _ _ _

4. Name at least 3 of the company present at the birth. _ _ _ _ _ _ _ _ _ _ _ _ _ _ _ _ _ _
    _

5. From which King did Jesus have to be descended? _ _ _ _ _ _ _ _ _ _ _ _ _ _ _ _ _ _ _

6. Who was His mother?
    _ _ _ _ _ _ _ _ _ _ _ _ _

7. Who was His Father?
    _ _ _ _ _ _ _ _ _ _ _

8. To which sect did His mother belong? _ _ _ _ _ _ _ _ _ _ _ _ _ _ _ _ _ _

9. How many Magi travelled to the place of the birth?
    _ _ _ _ _ _ _ _ _ _ _ _ _ _ _ _

10. What was their GPS / SatNav equivalent? _ _ _ _ _ _ _ _ _ _ _ _ _ _ _ _ _ _ _

11. Name 3 gifts that they brought. (The first Christmas gifts)
    _

12. Where did the Magi travel from? _ _ _ _ _ _ _ _ _ _ _ _ _ _ _ _ _ _

13. Who was the reigning king of Israel at this time?
    _ _ _ _ _ _ _ _ _ _ _ _ _ _ _ _

14. What gift did this king have in mind for the newborn?
    _

15. Thus, the family left quickly for a 'holiday' to where?
    _ _ _ _ _ _ _ _ _ _ _ _ _ _ _ _

16. Name their chosen form of transport.
    _ _ _ _ _ _ _ _ _ _ _ _ _ _ _ _

17. Why do you think the special day is called 'Christmas'?
    _
    _

My score is ___ / 17

(Answers overleaf.)

Quick Quiz around the Christmas Tree

Answers

Allow discussion or debate.

1. In which town was Jesus born?
    Bethlehem

2. Who was the Roman Emperor who decreed that all the world at this time should be taxed (or be part of a census)?
    Caesar Augustus

3. From which city in Galilee had the family travelled in accordance with the Emperor's decree? (They had to return to the place of their lineage.)
    Nazareth

4. Name at least 3 of the company present at the birth.
    Mary, Joseph, Jesus, Angels . . .

5. From which King did Jesus have to be descended?
    King David

6. Who was His mother?
    Mary

7. Who was His Father?
    Jehovah

8. To which sect did His mother belong?
    Essenes

9. How many Magi travelled to the place of the birth?
    3

10. What was their GPS / SatNav equivalent?
    A star

11. Name 3 gifts that they brought. (The first Christmas gifts)
    Gold, frankincense, myrrh, riches

12. Where did the Magi travel from?
    The East, probably Persia

13. Who was the reigning king of Israel at this time?
    King Herod

14. What gift did this king have in mind for the newborn?
    Killing Him *(Slaughter of the Innocents)*

15. Thus, the family left quickly for a 'holiday' to where?
    Egypt

16. Name their chosen form of transport.
    Donkey

17. Why do you think the special day is called 'Christmas'?

    (After Christ the Redeemer and the Mass to celebrate the birth)

THE FIRST CHRISTMAS

What do you really know?

What do you know about the first Christmas?

1. In which town was Jesus born?

   _____

2. Name at least 3 of the company present at His birth.

   _____

3. As foretold, from whom was he descended?

   _____

4. Who was His mother? _____

5. His Father? _____

6. To which sect did His mother belong?

   _____

7. How many Magi were there? _____

8. What GPS equivalent did the Magi use?

   _____

9. Name 3 gifts the Magi brought.

   _____

10. From where did the Magi come?

    _____

11. Who was the king at this time?

    _____

12. What gift did he have in mind for the newborn? _____

13. Not wanting this 'gift' from the king, the family took a hasty holiday. To where?

    _____

14. What form of transport did they most likely use? _____

15. Why is this day called Christmas?

    _____

HIDDEN WORDS from the CHRISTMAS STORY

Read this passage to find hidden words that are often heard in Christmas stories. Underline these and write below.

No one sets table to greet her or to arrange lights. Also, no magician or other odd man germinates ideas to get things started. But rosemary leaf locks a kind of botanical scribble over the hay that Beth le Hemmingway strewed around. Sadly, no big old welcome but do remember, 'pardon' key to humility.

The lady – she rode on a beast of burden – otherwise men would have offered help. The face of this person was glowing. No scowl was there. All sheep raised their heads. Others from afar came laden with gifts.

And so began the first Christmas.

_____
_____
_____
_____
_____

---------- *Cut along here* ----------

No one set**s table** to greet her or to arr**ange l**ights. Also, no **magi**cian or ot**her odd man ger**minates ideas to get things **star**ted. But rose**mary** lea**f locks** a kind of botanical s**crib**ble over the **hay** that **Beth le Hem**mingway strewed around. Sadly, no bi**g old** welcome but do remember, 'par**don' key** to humility.

The lady – s**he rod**e on a **beast** of burden – other**wise men** would have offered help. The face of this person was g**lowing**. No s**cowl** was there. All **sheep** raised their heads. Others from afar **came l**aden with **gifts**.

And so began the first **Christmas**.

Scores: 20+ Brilliant!; 15-19 Great!; 10-14 Well done; 5-9 Good try; Any score ☐

---

1. Bethlehem   2. Mary, Joseph, Jesus, cattle, angels   3. King David   4. Mary   5. Jehovah   6. Essenes
6. Three   8. A star   9. gold, frankincense, myrrh, riches   10. The East – probably Persia   11. Herod
12. Killing Him   13. Egypt   14. Donkey   15. After Christ, and the Mass to celebrate His birth

WORD FINDER

The letters in the circuit form one word. Your task is to identify that word and then to find as many words of 4 letters or more as you can. Each word must contain the central letter 'T'.

RULES: *You may NOT use people or place names, unless they are also used in our normal language.*
No plurals ending in 'S' are permitted unless this is also a word in another context.
Use letters one time only or in the abundance that they occur in the circuit only.

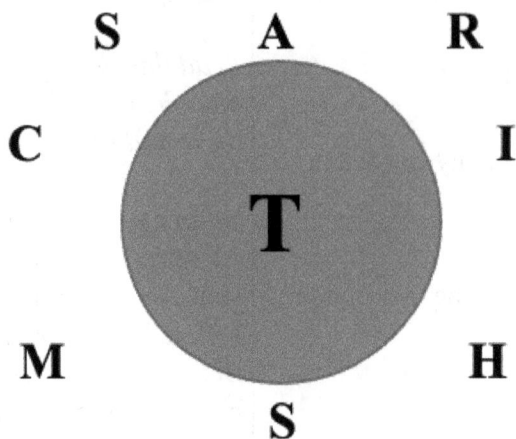

```
        S        A        R

    C                          I

                 T

    M                          H

                 S
```

I found these:-   The word is _ _ _ _ _ _ _ _ _ .

_____   _____   _____   _____

_____   _____   _____   _____

_____   _____   _____   _____

_____   _____   _____   _____

_____   _____   _____   _____

_____   _____   _____   _____

_____   _____   _____   _____

_____   _____   _____   _____

My score is ____ . □29 (□□□□); 24 – 28 (□□□□); 19 – 23 (□□□); 15-18 (□□); □ 14: (□).

_____*Possible Answers*_____

The word is **CHRISTMAS** .

ACTS, AITCH, *ARTIC*, ARTS, ASTI, CART, CAST, CHART, CHARTISM, CHAT, CHIT, CHRIST, CRISTA, HART, HIST, HITS, ITCH, MARIST, MART, MAST, MASTIC, MATH, MATHS, MATRIC, MIRTH, MISACT, MISCAST, MIST, SAITH, SCARTH, SCAT, SCHIST, SHIRT, SHIT, SITAR, SMART, SMARTISH, SMIT, SMITH, STAIR, STAIRS, STAR, STARCH, STASH, TACHISM, TARSI, THIS, TISH, TRAM, TRASH, TRIM, TSAR, TSARISM

'WAY TO GO!'

This is the 'left – right' decision-making game.

You will need an Emcee (reader) and numbered envelopes, one for each person sitting around the table. The highest number on the envelopes will match the number of people seated in the circle. For example, if there are 9 people, then number from 1 to 9.

Each person is to be given an envelope, following the numerical order. Everyone should be within easy reach of each other. Place whatever you choose in each envelope – a gift / a voucher / a pass or ticket to somewhere / a puzzle to solve / a certificate / something ridiculous . . .

When you hear the word 'right', move the envelope in front of you to in front of the person on your right. Similarly, if you hear 'left', place the envelope which is front of you to in front of the person on your left. Respond as quickly as you can.

*Remember you are '**giving**' to either left or right. Christmas is about **giving**.*

Let's begin.

This is the story of Mrs <u>Wright</u>, a teacher who was <u>right</u> into religious history, and her husband, Mr <u>Wright</u>, who felt quite <u>left</u> out of things because he wasn't <u>right</u> into that sphere of activity.

Mrs <u>Wright</u> decided to share the Christmas story with students who were <u>left</u> in her class in what was <u>left</u> of the school year. So that Mr <u>Wright</u> could come <u>right</u> on board with the project, the forth<u>right</u> Mrs <u>Wright</u> asked Mr <u>Wright</u> to <u>write</u> down the story. Now Mr <u>Wright</u> was <u>left</u>-handed but he now felt al<u>right</u> with this as he no longer felt <u>left</u> out of the fun.

Here is their version of the Christmas story:

Over 2,000 years ago, an angel came to tell a <u>right</u>eous girl called 'Mary' that she had been given the <u>right</u> to bring the Messiah, who had been <u>right</u>fully prophesied, into the human world. Mary decided this was al<u>right</u> and so the angel <u>left</u> and went <u>right</u> back to where he had come from. His mission was an out<u>right</u> success!

Now, at some time later when the child was to be born, 3 wisemen (Magi) spotted a wonderful star <u>right</u> over their heads. It was so unusual a sign that they grabbed their bags and camels and <u>left</u> <u>right</u> away to follow it. These 3 fellows were important so when they entered <u>right</u> into the territory of a tyrant ruler called Herod, this ruler had the 3 blokes brought to him so that he could stick his nose <u>right</u> into their business. Herod was a bit of a nasty type who <u>left</u> no one in doubt about the <u>right</u>s of kings.

So – back to the story.

Herod asked the Magi what <u>right</u> they had to ride their camels <u>right</u> onto his turf. They replied that they had <u>left</u> home to find the <u>right</u>ful heir to the kingdom. Herod, of course, took this to mean 'his'. Prophets had to <u>write</u> about this a long time ago so that people would know the <u>right</u> signs and the <u>right</u>ful heir to the kingdom (which was actually the kingdom of God).

Cunning old Herod told the Magi to come <u>right</u> back to him after they had found the <u>right</u> child. However, an angel stepped in and said this was not the <u>right</u> thing to do and so, after finding the <u>right</u>eous child and family, they <u>left</u> by another route.

All this <u>left</u> Herod pretty angry so he called in his <u>lieu</u>tenant (*pronounced 'left-tenant'*) to come up with a plan because he did not want any rivals to his <u>right</u>ful position. The plan was to get the <u>lieu</u>tenant's men <u>right</u> out and make sure there were no baby boys <u>left</u>. The <u>lieu</u>tenant <u>left</u> to get <u>right</u> on with this horrible job.

Meantime, back at the stable where the holy family was, the angel had kept the child <u>right</u> in his sights and so he told the baby's parents that they should have <u>left</u> <u>right</u> away.

So - they found a donkey and <u>left</u> <u>right</u> away so that the <u>lieu</u>tenant of Herod was <u>left</u> with a failed mission. Herod didn't know who the family was or that they had <u>left</u>. Years later, the family heard that old nasty Herod had <u>left</u> the land of the living and so they came <u>right</u> back. Then Jesus and his family got <u>right</u> on with their lives.

Mr <u>Wright</u> finished w<u>ri</u>ting this story and decided, like Mrs <u>Wright</u>, that this story was al<u>right</u> and he no longer felt <u>left</u> out!

THE END !

VARIATION OF GAME: *Christmas is also about 'getting'. Try the 'getting' version with rules reversed. When you hear 'right',* **TAKE** *from the right and when you hear 'left',* **TAKE** *from the left. Play this version straight after the first and enjoy the utter confusion.*

Now open the envelope that is now in front of you.

MYSTERY PARCEL IDEAS

for Christmas or celebrations

Select a gift of universal appeal to your family and guests.

Wrap the gift then select a question from the list or create one on the Christmas or Biblical theme and stick it on the parcel. Add a layer of wrapping paper and attach a different puzzle to the next layer. Continue the layers with questions.

TO PLAY: Have your Master of Ceremonies read the puzzle on the outer wrapping. Whoever answers correctly first is given the parcel, is to unwrap a layer, read the emerging new question / puzzle and pass the parcel to the one who successfully answers first. Play till someone receives the gift. Your Master of ceremonies should have an answer sheet.

SUGGESTIONS		ANSWERS
Name a Book of the Bible named after a woman	1.	Ruth / Judith / Ester
Think of 3 things disciples consumed at the Passover / Last Supper	2.	Unleavened bread, wine, water, lamb
What functional practice do Jews and Seventh Day Adventists have in common?	3.	Worship on the 7th day which is Saturday
How many commandments did Moses have on all the tablets of stone?	4.	20. He threw the first lot at the misbehaving crowd.
Whoever can name most of the 12 disciples deserves this parcel.	5.	Simon called Peter, Simon the Zealot, James (son of Zebedee), James (son of Alphaeus), John (not the Baptist), Andrew, Philip, Bartholomew, Matthew, Thomas, Jude Thaddeus, Judas Iscariot
What links frogs, mosquitoes, boils and hail?	6.	Plagues of Egypt
Name a gift brought by the Magi to the baby Jesus	7.	Gold, frankincense, myrrh, riches
What is greater than God, more evil than the devil and turns lead into gold?	8.	Nothing

11 Faithful Apostles	# The Apostle

The Apostle
Simon

11 Faithful Apostles

Peter

John - The Evangelist

& James, His Brother

Andrew

Philip

Thomas

Bartholomew

Matthew

James – Son of

Alphaeus

Simon The Zealot

Jude – Son of James
(Thaddaeus)

❖ Called Simon the 'Zealot' or 'Zealous'

❖ Of the Jews (from Cana in Galilee)

❖ Preached the Good News in Egypt

❖ Joined the Apostle Jude in Persia

❖ Martyred in Persia

Faith is free.

Faith is a gift.

Faith comes from God.

MATCH THE NUMBERS WITH THE APPROPRIATE

BIBLICAL PERSON / PLACE

(Answers overleaf)

BIBLICAL PERSON / PLACE	CHARACTERISTIC
___ Barabbas	1. Tentmaker
___ Sea of Galilee	2. Birthplace of Jesus
___ The Apostle Luke	3. Where walking on water witnessed
___ Pilate	4. Another fisherman
___ Mary	5. Tax collector
___ Jonah	6. Carpenter
___ Jesus	7. King of Judaea
___ Lazarus	8. Shouldered the cross for Christ
___ Joseph of Arimathaea	9. Governor
___ Simon called Peter	10. Insurrectionist and murderer
___ Simon from Cyrene	11. The Baptist
___ Herod	12. Wealthy member of Jewish Council
___ Thomas	13. From Magdala
___ Paul (Saul)	14. High Priest
___ Judas	15. Raised from grave by Christ
___ (Simon) Peter's brother	16. Inside info on anatomy of fish
___ John	17. Seen hanging around after crucifixion
___ Caiaphas	18. An Apostle (from region of Syria)
___ The Apostle Matthew	19. Apostle referred to as 'the rock'
___ Bethlehem	20. Not easily convinced

MATCH THE NUMBERS WITH THE APPROPRIATE

BIBLICAL PERSON / PLACE

Answers to

BIBLICAL PERSON / PLACE	CHARACTERISTIC
1. Paul (Saul)	1. Tentmaker (ACTS 18:3)
2. Bethlehem	2. Birthplace of Jesus
3. Sea of Galilee	3. Where walking on water witnessed
4. (Simon-) Peter's brother Andrew	4. Another fisherman
5. The Apostle Matthew	5. Tax collector
6. Jesus	6. Carpenter
7. Herod	7. King of Judaea
8. Simon from Cyrene	8. Shouldered the cross for Christ
9. Pilate	9. Governor
10. Barabbas	10. Insurrectionist and murderer
11. John	11. The Baptist
12. Joseph of Arimathaea	12. Wealthy member of Jewish Council
13. Mary	13. From Magdala
14. Caiaphas	14. High Priest
15. Lazarus	15. Raised from grave by Christ
16. Jonah	16. Inside info on anatomy of fish
17. Judas	17. Seen hanging around after crucifixion
18. The Apostle Luke	18. An Apostle (from region of Syria)
19. Simon called Peter	19. Apostle referred to as 'the rock'
20. Thomas	20. Not easily convinced

GOOD NEWS PREACHERS OF THE NEW TESTAMENT

The names of disciples and apostles and others who preached the Good News are hidden in this grid - forwards, backwards, vertically and diagonally. (Some letters overlap.) Find the names. There are 19 remaining letters which, in order of reading, hold a secret message.

Write the 'leftover' letters in order below the grid to uncover the secret message.

(Answers are overleaf.)

B	P	E	T	E	R	B	E	T	H	L
K	A	E	S	E	M	A	J	V	E	U
R	U	R	Y	E	K	U	D	L	B	A
A	L	E	T	H	A	D	D	E	U	S
M	A	T	T	H	E	W	O	M	S	T
Y	P	Y	H	T	O	M	A	S	T	A
T	I	J	O	U	L	J	O	E	E	N
I	L	E	M	C	A	N!	O	E	P	D
M	I	S	A	D	U	J	H	H	H	R
O	H	U	S	I	M	O	N	A	E	E
N	P	S	H	P	E	S	O	J	N	W

_ _ _ _ _ _   _ _ _   _ _ _ _ !

33

GOOD NEWS PREACHERS OF THE NEW TESTAMENT

Answers

Horizontal **Row** 1 – Peter; 2 – James (Apostle); 3 – Luke; 4 – Thaddeus; 5 – Matthew; 6 – Timothy; 9 – Judas (brother of James ACTS 1:13); 10 – Simon; 11 – Joseph (Barsabas ACTS 1:23): **Vertical Column** 1 – Mark, Timon (ACTS 6:5): 2 – Paul; Philip; 3 – Jesus; 4 – Thomas; 8 – Jude; John; 9 – James (ACTS 15:13); 10 – Stephen (first martyr); 11 – Saul (called Paul); Andrew **Diagonal** - Bartholomew:

B	P	E	T	E	R	B	E	T	H	L
K	A	E	S	M	E	A	J	V	E	U
R	U	R	R	Y	E	K	U	L	B	A
A	L	E	T	H	A	D	D	E	U	S
M	A	T	T	H	E	W	E	S	S	T
Y	P	Y	H	T	O	M	I	T	T	A
T	I	O	O	U	L	J	J	S	E	N
I	L	E	M	A	C	A	N!	Q	E	P	D
M	H	U	D	J	U	J	H	M	H	R
O	H	S	I	M	O	N	O	A	A	E
N	P	S	H	P	E	S	O	J	N	W

Secret Message: BE THE VERY BEST YOU CAN!

... / 21 Preachers

34

THERE ARE 13 WOMEN OF THE BIBLE HIDDEN IN THIS PARAGRAPH.

(Their names are in words or across words.)

Can you find them?

In truth, there is ever so many a female who cooks with rosemary and other herbs. Abigail's favourite is lime rabbit! After her bath, she bakes the best herb-flavoured rabbit. Standing for as long as she bakes makes her ache, legs and arms alike.

But, it's really diabolically edible! "Ah!" to find that recipe book.

With a tag or tab it has to be easy.

You need card or cash to buy a copy.

THEN text the order to reach Anna handling all sales.

Your book will soon be on the way!

Underline each name you find. Some are well known, others more obscure.

(Answers overleaf.)

ANSWERS TO '13 WOMEN OF THE BIBLE'

In t<u>ruth</u>, there is <u>ever</u> so many a female who cooks with rose<u>mary</u>

and other herbs. <u>Abigail</u>'s favourite is <u>lime rab</u>bit!

After her <u>bath, she ba</u>kes the best herb-flavoured rabbit. Standing

for as long as <u>she ba</u>kes makes he<u>r ache, l</u>egs and arms alike.

But, it's real<u>ly dia</u>bolically edib<u>le! "Ah</u>!" to find that recipe book.

With a tag or <u>tab it has</u> to be easy.

You need car<u>d or cas</u>h to buy a copy.

THEN text the order to reac<u>h Anna h</u>andling all sales.

Your book will soon be on the way!

1. Ruth
2. Eve
3. Mary
4. Abigail
5. Merab
6. Bathsheba
7. Sheba
8. Rachel
9. Lydia
10. Leah
11. Tabitha
12. Dorcas
13. Hannah

Score: ___ / 13

Book in!

Write the book of the bible beside each abbreviation.

Old Testament	New Testament
Is _____	
Ezr _____	Th _____
Jdt _____	Tm _____
Gn _____	Tt _____
Mi _____	Jn _____
Jb _____	Jm _____
Est _____	Mt _____
Ezk _____	Mk _____
Dn _____	Rv _____
Ex _____	Rm _____
Jon _____	P _____
Ob _____	Ph _____
Nb _____	Ac _____
K _____	Lk _____
Ps _____	Col _____
Jl _____	Co _____
Jos _____	Heb _____
Jg _____	Ga _____
Pr _____	Jude _____
S _____	Ep _____
Jr _____	Phm _____
Ml _____	Ws _____

The Lord's Prayer
(King James version:
Ryrie Study Bible. Matthew 6:9)

Our Father which art in Heaven,
Hallowed be thy name.
Thy kingdom come.
Thy will be done in earth,
As it is in heaven.
Give us this day our daily bread.
And forgive us our debts,
As we forgive our debtors.
And lead us not into temptation,
But deliver us from evil:
For thine is the kingdom, and
the power and the glory, for ever.
Amen

Proverbs

Better have little and with it virtue,
than great revenues and no right to
them.

The way of the lazy is strewn with
thorns, the path of the industrious
is a broad highway.

Kindly words are a honeycomb,
sweet to the taste, wholesome
to the body.

To mock the poor is to insult his
creator; he who laughs at distress
shall not go unpunished.

Pride goes before destruction,
a haughty spirit before a fall.

A friend is a friend at all times;
it is for adversity that a brother is
born.

The false witness shall not go
unpunished;
the man who utters lies will meet his
end.

Refer to the Contents page in a bible for best matches.

Answers page 44.

11 Faithful Apostles
Peter
John - The Evangelist
& James, His Brother
Andrew
Philip
Thomas
Bartholomew
Matthew
James – Son of
Alphaeus
Simon The Zealot
Jude – Son of James
(Thaddaeus)

The Apostle
John

Also called 'John the Evangelist'

❖ The only Apostle not martyred

❖ Brother of James

❖ Jewish fisherman

❖ Son of Zebedee and Salome

❖ From Galilee

❖ Disciple of John the Baptist

❖ Early follower of Christ

❖ Became the beloved disciple of Christ

❖ Preached with Peter (Samaria, probably Antioch, Ephesus and Rome)

❖ From Rome exiled to isle of Patmos

❖ At Patmos, where visions of The Book of Revelation called *Apocalypse* (Greek) were received;
Died Patmos late first century A.D.

Whose child is this?

Choose the child's parent / parents from the box and write the name / names in the space provided. Some names occur more than once, others not at all. Score 1 point for each parent you identify. Both parents may be represented.

Hannah	Sarah (Sarai)	Esther	Jesse
Isaac	Abraham	Jacob (Israel)	Lamech
Mary	Abigail	Eve	Solomon
Adam	Beryl	David	Zacharias
Hagar	Rebekah	Rachel	Leah
Phoebe	Jonah	Timothy	Elizabeth
Noah	Ezekiel	Bathsheba	Peter

1. Ishmael _____

2. Jacob (Israel) _____

3. John the Baptist _____

4. Rehoboam _____

5. Esau _____

6. Isaac _____

7. David _____

8. Cain _____

9. Samuel _____

10. Absolom _____

11. Jesus _____

12. Ham _____

13. Solomon _____

14. Joseph (Ruler in Egypt) _____

15. Seth _____

16. Abel _____

17. Benjamin _____

18. Judah _____

SCORES: ... / 30

Scored more than 1? Well done!

(Answers overleaf.)

Whose child is this?

1.	Ishmael	*Abraham & Hagar*
2.	Jacob (Israel)	*Isaac & Rebekah*
3.	John the Baptist	*Zacharias & Elizabeth*
4.	Rehoboam	*Solomon*
5.	Esau	*Isaac & Rebekah*
6.	Isaac	*Abraham & Sarah*
7.	David	*Jesse*
8.	Cain	*Adam & Eve*
9.	Samuel	*Hannah*
10.	Absolom	*David*
11.	Jesus	*Mary*
12.	Ham	*Noah*
13.	Solomon	*David & Bathsheba*
14.	Joseph (Ruler in Egypt)	*Jacob & Rachel*
15.	Seth	*Adam & Eve*
16.	Abel	*Adam & Eve*
17.	Benjamin	*Jacob & Rachel*
18.	Judah	*Jacob & Leah*

Unleavened Bread

(A tradition long kept)

Pizza oven cooking is probably as close to the original mode of cooking unleavened bread as exists today.

Try writing a recipe that would be practical for the people at the time of the Exodus.

Ingredients and instructions, with preliminaries, should be appropriate to the times.
Diagrams might be useful.

Design an oven that would have suited the Exodus times - nearly three and a half thousand years ago!

Matzoh – Unleavened Bread

Unleavened bread, that is, bread without yeast, is eaten during the Passover each year to commemorate the Exodus of the Israelites from Egypt. They left Egypt in haste and so had no time to wait for the yeast to cause the dough to rise.
Recipes for matzos are simple. There are quite a few on the internet. Choose one that suits your available equipment.

Ingredients:
2 $\frac{3}{4}$ cups plain flour
1 teaspoon fine salt (e.g. sea salt)
$\frac{1}{3}$ cup of olive oil
½ cup of water

Preheat oven to high.
Combine flour, oil and half the salt.
Blend mixture, adding a little water gradually until dough forms a soft, pliable ball. If it feels sticky, a little extra plain flour could be added.

Divide dough into 12 parts and, using a floured rolling pin, roll each one out until thin like a wafer.
Sprinkle sparingly with rest of salt. Press.
Place on baking paper and bake in oven or place on floured paper on heated pizza stone in pizza oven. The stone is pre-heated at a very high temperature for about ¾ hour.
Turn after a few minutes or when golden.

Remove when crisp. Cool.

Note: Temperatures in pizza oven are much higher. Therefore, cooking time will be much less (~ 15 minutes) than an ordinary oven. Try 15 – 20 minutes on high at 200⁰ C in the oven. Adjust if needed.
Remove from oven and cool on a rack.
You could keep some matzos plain and experiment with additives to the others e.g. herbs, spices, a very small amount of sugar (as sugar will quickly burn)

WHO SPOKE THESE WORDS?

Part 2

These words may sound familiar. Can you decide who is credited with uttering/writing them?

1. Never let the sun set on your anger. _____

2. For the moment your greeting reached my ears, the child in my womb leapt for joy. _____

3. For I testify unto every man that heareth the words of the prophecy of this book; if any man shall add unto these things, God shall add unto him the plagues that are written in this book. _____

4. Not even the Archangel Michael, when he was engaged in argument with the devil about the corpse of Moses, dared to denounce him in the language of abuse; all he said was, "Let the Lord correct you!" _____

5. Can a mother forget the baby at her breast, and have no compassion on the child she has borne? Though she may forget, I will not forget you! See, I have engraved you on the palms of my hands. _____

6. The spirit is willing but the flesh is weak. _____

7. Get up, take the child and his mother with you and go back to the land of Israel, for those who wanted to kill the child are dead. _____

8. All the commandments . . . are summed up in this single command, you must love your neighbour as yourself. Love is the only thing that cannot hurt your neighbour; that is why it is the answer to every one of the commandments. _____

9. What is this that thou hast done unto me? Why didst thou not tell me that she was thy wife? _____

10. I have made a light for the nations so that my salvation may reach the ends of the earth. _____

11. They have no wine. (*The wine provided had run out.*) _____

12. If you are the king of the Jews, save yourself. _____

13. You should not write 'King of the Jews', but 'This man said: I am King of the Jews'. _____

14. There are many things that Jesus did. If all were written down, the world itself, I suppose, would not hold all the books that would have to be written. _____

15. My soul doth magnify the Lord; and my spirit hath rejoiced in God my Saviour. _____

My score is . . . / 15

(Answers overleaf.)

WHO SPOKE THESE WORDS?

Answers for Part 2

Paul Ephesians 4:27	1. Never let the sun set on your anger.
Elizabeth Luke 1:44	2. For the moment your greeting reached my ears, the child in my womb leapt for joy.
John (the Disciple) Revelation ; Epilogue	3. For I testify unto every man that heareth the words of the prophecy of this book, if any man shall add unto these . . .
Jude Letter of Jude	4. Not even the Archangel Michael, when he was engaged in argument with the devil . . .
Isaiah Isaiah 49:15	5. Can a mother forget the baby at her breast, and have no compassion on the child she has borne? . . .
Jesus Mark 14:38,39	6. The spirit is willing but the flesh is weak.
Angel of the Lord Matthew 2:20	7. Get up, take the child and his mother with you and go back to the land of Israel, for those who wanted to kill the child . . .
Paul Romans 13:9	8. All the commandments are summed up in this single command: You must love your neighbour as yourself.
Pharaoh to Abraham Genesis 12:18	9. What is this that thou hast done unto me? Why didst thou not tell me that she was thy wife?
God / Jehovah Acts 13:47	10. I have made a light for the nations so that my salvation may reach the ends of the earth.
Mary Mother of Jesus John 2:4	11. They have no wine. *(The wine provided had run out.)*
Roman soldiers Luke 23:37	12. If you are the king of the Jews, save yourself.
Chief Priests John 19:21	13. You should not write 'King of the Jews', but 'This man said: I am King of the Jews'.
John (the Disciple) John 21:25	14. There are many things that Jesus did. If all were written down, the world itself, would not hold all the books . . .
Mary Mother of Jesus Luke 1:46	15. My soul doth magnify the Lord; and my spirit hath rejoiced in God my Saviour.

MULTIPLE-AWARD QUICK QUIZ

One award / prize for the quickest to provide a correct answer.
Suggested responses are not exhaustive.

Instructions: *(The Master of Ceremonies reads from this page.)*

*Think of a character(-s) and event **OR** character(-s) and circumstance
associated with each of these animals mentioned in the Bible.
There are 11 animals to consider. The first one to associate is 'Lion'.*

1. **LION**   Daniel in lions' den . . .

2. **SNAKE**   Eve in Garden of Eden; Moses with Pharaoh's High Priests . . . .

3. **CAMEL**   The Magi to the manger; Jesus and parable of rich man

4. **DONKEY**   Mary to Egypt; Jesus riding into Jerusalem . . . .

5. **PIGS**   Prodigal son as swineherd; Jesus casting evil spirits into pigs which ran

    over a cliff . . .

6. **DOVE**   Noah and the Ark, at the end of the Great Flood; Jesus and

    circumcision offering . . .

7. **SHEEP**   David with flock; offering at Passover . . . .

8. **WHALE**   Jonah in storm

9. **FISH**   Feeding the masses; Sea of Galilee and disciples . . . .

10. **LOCUSTS**   John the Baptist in the desert; 8th plague of Egypt . . .

11. **GOLDEN CALF** False worship in the desert after the Exodus . . .

SOME PLANTS AND ANIMALS
of the Bible

Choose the most appropriate answer from the box to fit the clues following.
Words in the box are used once only.

FRANKINCENSE	LOCUSTS	WHALE	SHEEP
FROGS	OLIVE BRANCH	HEMLOCK	DOVE
LION	DONKEY	POMEGRANATE	SWINE
UNICORN	HYSSOP	EAGLE	APPLE
SERPENT	COCK / ROOSTER	DROMEDARIES	DODO

1. Carried Jesus into Jerusalem _____

2. The food Eve couldn't resist *(in popular representations)* _____

3. Sometimes burnt in prayer time _____

4. Symbol of the Holy Spirit _____

5. Included in John the Baptist's desert diet _____

6. Was heard when Peter denied knowing Jesus three times _____

7. Unusual accommodation chosen for Jonah_____

8. Animal likened to Tribe of Judah _____

9. Embroidered, with a golden bell, on the priestly robe of Aaron _____

10. The second plague brought upon Pharaoh *(Exodus 8:6)* _____

11. Part of a shrub symbolizing peace _____

12. *(Hosea 10:4)* A dangerous plant to find amongst your crops _____

13. The creature described as having tempted Eve _____

14. *(Luke 15:15)* The prodigal son fed these animals after squandering his inheritance _____

15. *(John 19:29)* A branch of this supported the vinegar-soaked sponge held to the mouth of the crucified Jesus _____

16. *(Revelations 12:14)* Its wings carried the woman into the safety of the wilderness _____

17. *(1 Samuel 16:11)* David, son of Jesse, was in charge of these animals

_____

18. *(Numbers 23:22)* A mythical creature said to have great strength

_____

19. *(Judges 10:1)* A name shared with an extinct bird and an early father / grandfather of a Judge of Israel _____

20. The wealth-laden camels from Sheba *(Isaiah 60:6)* _____

TOTAL CORRECT: ... / 20

(Answers overleaf.)

QUICK RECALL

The number '7' signifies 'completeness'.

Find examples of the number '7' occurring in the Book 'Revelation'.

When is '7' significant in other parts of the bible?

Find examples of the number '12' in 'Revelation'.

What other examples of '12' can you think of in the rest of the Bible?

ANSWERS TO "SOME PLANTS AND ANIMALS OF THE BIBLE"

1.	Carried Jesus into Jerusalem	*donkey*
2.	The food Eve couldn't resist *(in popular representations)*	*apple*
3.	Sometimes burnt in prayer time	*frankincense*
4.	Symbol of the Holy Spiri	*dove*
5.	Included in John the Baptist's desert diet	*locusts (honey locusts?)*
6.	Was heard when Peter denied knowing Jesus three times	*cock / rooster*
7.	Unusual accommodation chosen for Jonah	*whale*
8.	Animal likened to Tribe of Judah	*lion*
9.	Embroidered, with a golden bell, on the priestly robe of Aaron	*pomegranate*
10.	The second plague brought upon Pharaoh (Exodus 8:6)	*frogs*
11.	Part of a shrub symbolizing peace	*olive branch*
12.	(Hosea 10:4) A dangerous plant to find amongst your crops	*hemlock*
13.	The creature described as having tempted Eve	*serpent*
14.	(Luke 15:15) The prodigal son fed these animals after squandering his inheritance	*swine*
15.	(John 19:29) A branch of this supported the vinegar-soaked sponge held to the mouth of the crucified Jesus	*hyssop*
16.	(Revelations 12:14) Its wings carried the woman into the safety of the wilderness	*eagle*
17.	(1 Samuel 16:11) David, son of Jesse, was in charge of these animals	*sheep*
18.	(Numbers 23:22) A mythical creature said to have great strength	*unicorn (In some versions of the bible, the horned animal is recorded as an ox.)*
19.	(Judges 10:1) A name shared with an extinct bird and an early father / grandfather of a Judge of Israel	*dodo*
20.	The wealth-laden camels from Sheba (Isaiah 60:6)	*dromedaries*

Easy Easter Exercise!

Locate 20 Lenten words in this grid. Draw a line through each you find and tick off each on the list below. 6 letters remain. What word do they make?

C	C	J	E	S	U	S	L	H	N
A	R	E	E	J	U	D	A	S	I
L	O	R	O	M	A	N	S	A	R
V	S	U	P	P	E	R	T	C	D
A	S	S	A	U	G	U	R	Y	E
R	P	A	S	S	O	V	E	R	H
Y	V	L	P	I	L	A	T	E	N
B	R	E	A	D	A	E	N	N	A
T	O	M	B	E	N	I	W	E	S
C	U	P	R	A	G	E	N	I	V

(A)	AUGURY	**(G)**	GOLAN	**(P)**	PASSOVER	**(V)**	VINEGAR
(B)	BREAD	**(I)**	IDEA		PILATE	**(W)**	WINE
(C)	CALVARY	**(J)**	JESUS	**(R)**	ROMANS		
	CROSS		JUDAS	**(S)**	SANDHEDRIN		
	CUP		JERUSALEM		SUPPER		
	CYRENE	**(L)**	LAST	**(T)**	TOMB		

The Mystery Word is

_ _ _ _ _ _

(Answers overleaf.)

47

Answer check sheet for **Easy Easter Exercise!**

C	C	J	E	S	U	S	L	H	H	N
A	R	E	E	J	U	D	A	S	I	I
L	O	R	O	M	A	N	S	A	R	R
V	S	U	P	P	E	R	T	C	C	D
A	S	S	A	U	G	U	R	Y	E	E
R	P	A	S	S	O	V	E	R	H	H
Y	V	L	P	I	L	A	T	E	N	N
B	R	E	A	D	A	E	N	N	A	A
T	O	M	B	E	N	I	W	E	S	S
C	U	P	R	A	G	E	N	I	V

Mystery Word: HEAVEN

ANSWERS to 'Book in!' (page 32)

<u>Old</u> **Testament**: **Is** Isaiah; **Ezr** Ezra; **Jdt** Judith; **Gn** Genesis; **Mi** Micah; **Jb** Job; **Est** Ester; **Ezk** Ezekiel; **Dn** Daniel; **Ex** Exodus; **Jon** Jonah; **Ob** Obadiah; **Nb** Numbers; **K** Kings; **Ps** Psalms; **Jl** Joel; **Jos** Joshua; **Jg** Judges; **Pr** Proverbs; **S** Samuel; **Jr** Jeremiah; **Ml** Malachi.

<u>New</u> **Testament:** **Th** Thessalonians; **Tm** Timothy; **Tt** Titus; **Jn** John; **Jm** James; **Mt** Matthew; **Mk** Mark; **Rv** Revelation; **Rm** Romans; **P** Peter; **Ph** Philippians; **Ac** Acts; **LK** Luke; **Col** Colossians; **Co** Corinthians; **Heb** Hebrews; **Ga** Galatians; **Jude** Jude; **Ep** Ephesians; **Phm** Philemon; **Ws** Wisdom (not in all bibles).

EASTERTIDE CROSSWORD

Note: The double line border around square 11 separates 2 answers vertically and horizontally.

Across
1. Son of God ... His Name?
6. The body of Elders, Priests and Scribes
7. First disciple to see Jesus' empty tomb
10. Roman soldiers cast _ _ _ _ for Jesus' clothing
12. Animal sacrificed at Passover time
14. This blocked entrance to burial place
15. Disciples drank wine and _ _ _ bread in His Memory

Down
1. He came from Arimathaea
2. Jesus was 'without _ _ _'
3. Weapon that pierced the side of Jesus 4.
From 6th to 9th hour _____ fell over earth
5. 2 appeared to women outside empty burial
6. Jesus' body was placed in a _ _ _ _
9. Pontius P - - - - e (Complete this word)
10. It crowed thrice after Peter's denial
11. Scripture says 'not one _ _ _ _ would be broken
13. _ _ _ y was the name of 2 women who first came to Jesus' burial place

(Answers overleaf.)

49

ANSWERS TO EASTERTIDE CROSSWORD

	J¹	**E**	**S**²	**U**	**S**³		**D**⁴		
	O		**I**		**P**		**A**		**A**⁵
	S⁶	**A**	**N**	**H**	**E**	**D**	**R**	**I**	**N**
	E				**A**		**K**		**G**
	P⁷	**E**	**T**⁸	**E**	**R**		**N**		**E**
	H		**O**				**E**		**L**
I⁹ ⁽ᴾ⁾			**M**		**C**¹⁰	**A**	**S**	**T**	**B**¹¹
L¹²	**A**	**M**¹³	**B**		**O**		**S**		**O**
A		**A**			**C**				**N**
T ⁽ᴱ⁾		**R**¹⁴	**O**	**C**	**K**		**A**¹⁵	**T**	**E**

'Man does not live on bread alone but on every word that comes from the mouth of God.'

'I will speak to you in parables and expound things hidden since the foundation of the world.'

WHAT WAS THEIR OCCUPATION?

Enter their <u>first</u>- mentioned / earliest 'occupation'.   *(What were they?)*

1. The Apostle Matthew   _____

2. Jesus the Nazarene   _____

3. Barabbas (who gained his freedom
in exchange for that of Jesus)   _____

4. Simon called Peter   _____

5. Herod   _____

6. Caiaphas   _____

7. The brothers James and John (sons
of Zebedee)   _____

8. The Sadducees   _____

9. Octavian (Augustus)   _____

10. Pontius Pilate   _____

11. Saul called Paul   _____

12. Melchizedek   _____

13. Uriah the Hittite   _____

14. David   _____

TOTAL SCORE: ... / 14

WHAT WAS THEIR OCCUPATION?

Answer Sheet

1.	The Apostle Matthew	*Publican / Tax collector*	*(Matthew 10:4)*
2.	Jesus the Nazarene	*Carpenter*	*(Matthew 13:55)*
3.	Barabbas (who gained his freedom in exchange for that of Jesus)	*Murderer / Criminal*	*(Luke 23:19)*
4.	Simon called Peter	*Fisherman*	*(Mark 1:15,16)*
5.	Herod	*King of Judaea*	*(Acts 12:1)*
6.	Caiaphas	*High Priest*	*(John 11:49)*
7.	The brothers James and John (sons of Zebedee)	*Fishermen*	*(Mark 1:19)*
8.	The Sadducees	*Keepers of the Law*	*(Acts 4:1,2)*
9.	Octavian (Augustus)	*Emperor of Rome*	*(Luke 2:1)*
10.	Pontius Pilate	*Governor*	*(Matthew 27:2)*
11.	Saul called Paul	*Tentmaker*	*(Acts 18:3)*
12.	Melchizedek	*King (of Salem)*	*(Genesis 14:18)*
13.	Uriah the Hittite	*Soldier*	*(2 Samuel 11:3-17)*
14.	David	*Shepherd*	*(1 Samuel 16:11-13)*

TOTAL SCORE: ... / 14

(Jude:20)   A call to persevere: "Remember what the apostles of our Lord Jesus Christ foretold. They said to you, 'In the last times there will be scoffers who will follow their own desires..........' These are the men who divide you, who follow mere natural instincts and do not have the Spirit."

A Quiz for Eastertide

Let's not forget the true Easter story!

1. How many men sat at table for the Last Supper? _____

2. Why has it been called The Last Supper? _____

3. This ceremonial meal is also called _____

4. What was it originally a commemoration of? _____

5. Where did the Last Supper take place (town)? _____

6. What was instituted at this particular meal? _____

7. Traditionally, this meal marked the beginning of The Feast of Unleavened Bread. For how many days does this feast last? _____

8. a. What ingredient does this bread lack? _____
    b. Why? _____

9. Suggest anything else, besides bread, that would have been on the table.
    _____

10. Who was 'the beloved disciple' sitting next to Jesus? _____

11. To whom was Jesus referring when he said 'Woe unto that man by whom the Son of man is betrayed! It had been better for that man if he had not been born.' _____

12. Jesus did not identify the 'betrayer' by name but by action at the table. What was this sign? _____

13. How did the 'betrayer' expect to profit by his actions? _____
    _____

14. Complete this: *For this is my blood of the new testament which is shed for many for*
    _____

15. To which Mount did the group walk after finishing supper? _____
    _____

My score _____ **/ 16**   **Well done!**

(Answers overleaf.)

53

Answers to
A Quiz for Eastertide

1. How many men sat at table for the Last Supper?   *13 – Jesus plus the 12*

2. Why has it been called The Last Supper?   *It was the living Jesus' last meal*

3. This ceremonial meal is also called?   *The Passover (meal)*

4. What was it originally a commemoration of?   *The Israelites meal before Exodus; the Angel of Death passed over the homes marked with the blood of the lamb*

5. Where did the Last Supper take place (town)?   *Bethany (entry to Jerusalem later)*

6. What was instituted at this particular meal?   *The Eucharist / Holy Communion*

7. Traditionally, this meal marked the beginning of The Feast of Unleavened Bread. For how many days does this feast last?   *7 days*

8. a. What ingredient does this bread lack?   *Leaven/yeast*
   b. Why?   *At the time of Exodus, no time to wait for bread to rise / God's instruction*

9. Suggest anything else, besides bread, that would have been on the table.   *roast lamb; bitter herbs; wine*

10. Who was 'the beloved disciple' sitting next to Jesus?   *John*

11. To whom was Jesus referring when he said 'Woe unto that man by whom the Son of man is betrayed! It had been better for that man if he had not been born.'   *Judas Iscariot*

12. Jesus did not identify the 'betrayer' by name but by action at the table. What was this sign?   *He dipped his hand in the dish at the same time as Jesus*

13. How did the 'betrayer' expect to profit by his actions?   *30 pieces of silver*

14. Complete this: *For this is my blood of the new testament which is shed for many for* **the forgiveness of sins**

15. To which Mount did the group walk after finishing supper?   *Mount of Olives*

PROPHESIES

'The Lord thy God will raise up unto thee a Prophet from the midst of thee, of thy brethren, like unto me, unto Him ye shall hearken ... and will put my words in his mouth, and he shall speak unto them all that I shall command him.'

From (Moses) Deuteronomy 18:15-17

'Look, I am going to send my messenger before you;
He will prepare your way before you.'

From (John the Baptist quoting scripture) Matthew 11:10

'And there shall come forth a root out of the stem of Jesse ...
and the spirit of the Lord shall rest upon him.'

From Isaiah 11:1

'I will also give a light to the Gentiles;
that thou mayest be my salvation unto the end of the Earth.'

From Isaiah 49:6

'But thou, Bethlehem Ephratah, though thou be little among the thousands of Judah, yet out of thee shall come forth unto me that is to be ruler in Israel; whose goings forth have been from of old, from everlasting.   Therefore will he give them up, until the time that she travaileth hath brought forth: then the remnant of his brethren shall return unto the children of Israel.'

From Micah 5:1; Matthew 2:6

'The virgin will conceive and give birth to a son
and they will call him Immanuel.'

From Isaiah 7:14

'For unto us a child is born, unto us a son is given, and the government shall be upon his shoulder, and his name shall be called Wonderful, Counsellor, The 'mighty' God, The Everlasting Father, The Prince of Peace ... upon the throne of David'

From Isaiah 9:6

P R O P H E S I E S

'Here is my servant whom I have chosen,
my beloved, the favourite of my soul.
I will endow him with my spirit,
and he shall proclaim the true faith to the nations.'
From Matthew 15:8 (The prophet Isaiah)

'It was the stone rejected by the builders that became the keystone.
This was the Lord's doing and it is wonderful to see.'
From Matthew 21:42 (citing Scripture)

'Say to the daughter of Zion:
Look, your king comes to you;
he is humble, he rides on a donkey
and on a colt, the foal of a beast of burden.'
From Matthew 21:5 (citing Scripture)

'He is despised and rejected of men ...
He was wounded for our transgressions.
He was bruised for our iniquities.
He was oppressed ... yet he opened not his mouth; he is brought as a
lamb to the slaughter ....'
From Isaiah 53: 3

'He took our sicknesses away and carried our diseases for us.'
From Matthew 8:17 (The prophet, Isaiah)

'And he bore the sin of many, and made intercession for the
transgressors.'
From Isaiah 53:12

'Therefore I say unto you, The Kingdom of God shall be taken from
you, and given to a nation bringing forth the fruits thereof.'
From Matthew 21:43 (Words of Jesus)

'I saw in the night visions, and, behold, one like the Son of Man came
with the clouds of heaven and came to the Ancient of Days (i.e. God as
Judge) ... and there was given to Him dominion, and glory, and a
kingdom, that all people, nations, and languages should serve Him: His
dominion which shall not pass away, and His kingdom that which shall
not be destroyed.'
From Daniel 7:13

LENTEN CROSSWORD

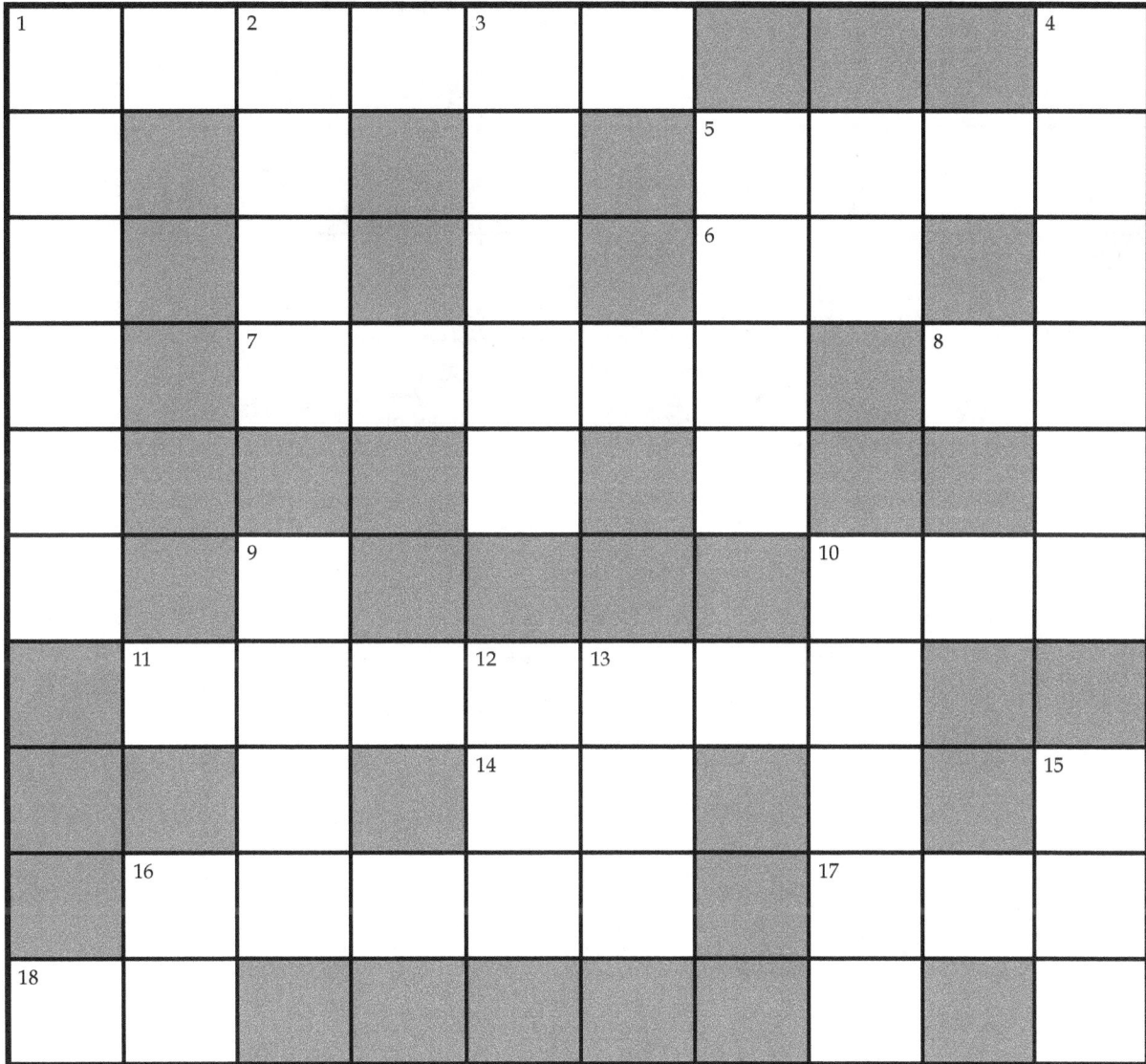

ACROSS

1. Last name of 'Pontius'
5. Mother of Jesus
6. Metal in coins in betrayal of Jesus by Judas (chemical symbol)
7. Food shared at the Last Supper
8. 'Jesus _ _ the Word made Flesh'
10. Jesus said '.. . and drink this _ _ _'
11. Liquid offered to Jesus on the Cross
14. 'Gol_ _ otha' meaning 'the place of a skull'
16. Jesus was taken before King _ _ _ _ _
17. Pilate said he found no _ _ _ in Jesus
18. '_ _ N T' is the period leading up to Easter and Passover

DOWN

1. Describes an unbeliever
2. Animal commonly sacrificed
3. Number of crosses at Jesus' Crucifixion site
4. A branch of this held what was offered to the dying Jesus
5. Thorny stems were _ _ _ _ into the crown of thorns
9. Beverage shared at The Last Supper
12. Indicates 'one's conscious thinking'
13. Jehovah, _ _ _ of Creation
15. Followers of Christ are united in _ _ _ body

(Answers overleaf.)

LENTEN CROSSWORD

P¹	I	L²	A	T³	E				H⁴
A		A		H		M⁵	A	R	Y
G		M		R		A⁶	G		S
A		B⁷	R	E	A	D		I⁸	S
N				E		E			O
S		W⁹					C¹⁰	U	P
	V¹¹	I	N	E¹²	G¹³	A	R		
		N		G¹⁴	O		O		O¹⁵
	H¹⁶	E	R	O	D		S¹⁷	I	N
L¹⁸	E						S		E

Psalm 23: The Divine Shepherd

The Lord is my shepherd, I shall not want.
He makes me lie down in green pastures.
He leads me beside still waters.
He restores my soul.
He leads me in right paths for His name's sake.
Even though I walk through the darkest valley,

I fear no evil for You are with me.
Your rod and Your staff – they comfort me.
You prepare a table for me in the presence of my enemies.
You anoint my head with oil.
My cup overflows.
Surely goodness and mercy shall follow me all the days of my life,
and I shall dwell in the house of the Lord my whole life long.

11 Faithful Apostles	# The Apostle

11 Faithful Apostles

Peter

John - The Evangelist

& James, His Brother

Andrew

Philip

Thomas

Bartholomew

Matthew

James – Son of

Alphaeus

Simon The Zealot

Jude – Son of James
(*Thaddaeus*)

The Apostle
James

❖ Brother of John the Evangelist

❖ Son of Zebedee and Salome

❖ From Galilee

❖ Fisherman with Peter, Andrew and John

❖ Witness to many miracles

❖ The first Apostle to die for Christ

❖ A martyr: beheaded by Herod Agrippa 1 in A.D. 42 or 44

❖ Buried in Jerusalem

❖ Relics said to have been moved to Compostela, Spain in A.D. 830 approx.

11 Faithful Apostles

Peter

John - The Evangelist

& James, His Brother

Andrew

Philip

Thomas

Bartholomew

Matthew

James – Son of

Alphaeus

Simon The Zealot

Jude – Son of James
(Thaddaeus)

The Apostle
Thomas

Also known as Didymus meaning 'twin'

❖ Has been called 'Doubting Thomas' for reserving his belief in the risen Christ until he was able to see Him physically

❖ Thereafter devoted himself to preaching the Good News

❖ Thought to have preached in Persia and India

❖ Possibly martyred in India

❖ Relics brought to Abruzzi, Italy

'You believe because you can see me. Happy are those who have not seen and yet believe.' *(Jesus to Thomas)*

'Go out to the whole world; proclaim the Good News to all creation. He who believes and is baptized will be saved . . . .'

ALPHABET OF BIBLE BOOKS

Match the name of an Old or New Testament book with letters of the alphabet. Some letters have multiple matches. Circle letters with no match. There are 8 of these. Which 2 of these circled letters do not appear in any of the Book's names?

A _____   N _____

B _____   O _____

C _____   P _____

D _____   Q _____

E _____   R _____

F _____   S _____

G _____   T _____

H _____   U _____

I _____   V _____

J _____   W _____

K _____   X _____

L _____   Y _____

M _____   Z _____

I found . . . books of the Bible.   The 8 letters without a match were: . . .

Which 2 letters do not appear in the names of any Bible Book?   _____   _____

(Checklist overleaf.)

Checklist for ALPHABET OF BIBLE BOOKS

A   Amos, (The) Acts
      (or 'According to 4 Gospels)

B

C   Chronicles, Corinthians,
      Colossians

D   Deuteronomy, Daniel

E   Exodus, Ezra, Esther,
      Ecclesiastes, Ezekiel, Ephesians

F

G   Genesis, Galatians

H   Hosea, Habakkuk, Haggai,
      Hebrews

I   Isaiah

J   Joshua, Judges, Job, Jeremiah,
      Joel, Jonah, John, James, Jude

K   Kings

L   Leviticus, Lamentations, Luke

M   Micah, Malachi, Matthew, Mark

N   Numbers, Nehemiah, Nahum

O   Obadiah

P   Psalms, Proverbs, Philippians,
      Philemon, Peter

Q

R   Ruth, Romans, Revelation

S   Samuel, (Song of) Solomon

T   The Acts, Thessalonians,
      Timothy, Titus

U

V

W

X

Y

Z   Zephaniah, Zechariah

Letters with no match: **B, F, Q, U, V, W, X, Y**

Letters which do not occur at all: **F** and **Q**

How many books of the bible can you name? How many can you name in the order of their occurrence? What is the first book? The last book? Which were named after kings? . . . .

WHO SPOKE THESE WORDS? Part 3

These words may sound familiar. Can you decide who is credited with uttering/writing them?

1. Fight the good fight . . . _____

2. Give back to Caesar what belongs to Caesar – and to God what belongs to God.
_____

3. Good Master, what must I do to inherit eternal life? _____

4. Saul, Saul, why are you persecuting me? _____

5. There are many rooms in my Father's house; if there were not, I should have told you.
_____

6. You may be quite sure that in the last days there are going to be some difficult times.
People will be self-centred and grasping; boastful; arrogant and rude; disobedient to
their parents; ungrateful; irreligious; heartless and unappeasable; they will be slanderers,
profligates, savages and enemies of everything that is good . . . _____

7. 'Our Father who art in Heaven,   Hallowed be thy name.   Thy Kingdom come. Thy
will be done on Earth as it is in Heaven.   Give us this day our daily bread and forgive
us our trespasses AS we forgive those who trespass against us. And lead us not into
temptation but deliver us from evil . . .' _____

8. We are in difficulties on all sides, but never cornered; we see no answer to our problems,
but never despair; we have been persecuted, but never deserted; knocked down, but
never killed. _____

9. When I was a child, I used to talk like a child, and think like a child, and argue like a
child, but now I am a man, all childish things are put behind me. _____

10. And this is the writing that was written, ME'NE, MENE, TE'KEL, UPHAR'SIN. This is
the interpretation of the thing; ME'NE; God hath numbered thy kingdom and finished it.
_____

11. And I __ __ __ __ saw the holy city, new Jerusalem, coming down from God out of
Heaven, prepared as a bride adorned for her husband.

12. Behold the fire and the wood, but where is the lamb for the burnt offering? _____

13. Behold, Esau, my brother is a hairy man, and I am a smooth man. _____

14. For, behold, we were binding sheaves in the field, and, lo, my sheaf arose, and also stood
upright; and, behold, your sheaves stood round about, and made obeisance to my sheath.
_____

15. I will work for you for 7 years to win your younger daughter, Rachel. _____

My score is _____ / 15

(Answers overleaf.)

WHO SPOKE THESE WORDS?

Answers for Part 2

Paul (to Timothy) 1 Timothy 6:12	1. Fight the good fight . . .
Jesus Mark 12:17	2. Give back to Caesar what belongs to Caesar – and to God what belongs to God.
Young wealthy man (to Jesus) Mark 10:17	3. Good Master, what must I do to inherit eternal life?
Jesus Acts 26:14	4. Saul, Saul, why are you persecuting me?
Jesus John 14:2	5. There are many rooms in my Father's house; if there were not ..
Paul (to Timothy) 2 Timothy 2:3	6. You may be quite sure that in the last days there are going to be some difficult times. People will be self-centred and grasping...
Jesus Matthew 6:10	7. 'Our Father who art in Heaven, Hallowed be thy name. Thy Kingdom come. Thy will be done on Earth . . . .'
Paul (in Macedonia) 2 Corinthians 4:7	8. We are in difficulties on all sides, but never cornered; we see no answer to our problems, but never despair . . .
Paul 1 Corinthians 13:11	9. When I was a child, I used to talk like a child, and think like a child, and argue like a child, but now I am a man, all childish things are put behind me.
Daniel (to Belshazzar) Daniel 5:25	10. And this is the writing that was written, ME'NE, MENE, TE'KEL, UPHAR'SIN. This is the interpretation of the thing...
John (Disciple) Revelation 21:2	11. And I __ __ __ __ saw the holy city, new Jerusalem, coming down from God out of Heaven . . . .
Isaac (to Abraham, his father) Genesis 22:7	12. Behold the fire and the wood, but where is the lamb for the burnt offering?
Jacob (to his mother, Rebekah) Genesis 27:11	13. Behold, Esau, my brother is a hairy man, and I am a smooth man.
Joseph (to his brothers) Genesis 37:7	14. For, behold, we were binding sheaves in the field, and, lo......
Jacob (to Laban) Genesis 29:18	15. I will work for you for 7 years to win your younger daughter, Rachel

11 Faithful Apostles

Peter

John - The Evangelist

& James, His Brother

Andrew

Philip

Thomas

Bartholomew

Matthew

James – Son of Alphaeus

Simon The Zealot

Jude – Son of James
(Thaddaeus)

The Apostle
Phillip

❖ Born Bethsaida in Galilee

❖ Next after Andrew and Peter to join Christ

❖ Witness to many miracles

❖ Preached the Good News gospel in Phrygia and likely in Greece

❖ Martyred in Hierapolis

❖ Relics now rest in Rome

It was the stone rejected by the builders
that became the keystone.
This was the Lord's doing
and it is wonderful to see.
Matthew 21:42

Topic for this Quick Quiz is pre-advised. Score 1 point each correct answer.

"The Exodus" After 430 years in exile

1.   From which country did the Exodus take place? _____

2.   What was the title of this country's ruler?_____

3a.   Who were the people emigrating? _____

b.   How did they come to be in this land in the first place? _____

_____

c.   Why did the Ruler resist their departing? _____

4a.   Name the leader or advocate for the people of the Exodus. _____

b.   This man was highly educated, which was unusual. How would this have

occurred? _____

c.   Who was his older brother? _____ (He was 80 yrs ; brother 83 yrs)

d.   What was his brother's occupation?_____

e.   The brother carried a _____ when called upon to show God's might.

5.   *"Let my people go that they may serve me."*
    But, the Ruler would not! *So* - plague after plague afflicted the country.

a.   How many plagues were there? _____

b.   The last was the most terrible. What was it? _____

_____

6. Is anyone clever enough to name the 10 plagues in order? (Bonus 9 points)

1. _____   2. _____   3. _____
4. _____   5. _____   6. _____
7. _____   8. _____   9. _____
10. _____

7. The plagues affected man and beast alike, the Exodus people being spared.

What beasts / animals would have provided for the needs of the peoples of that land? _____

_____

8. Think of any preparation for the Exodus the departing tribes were told to

undertake. _____

_____

9a. Through which sea did the Exodus pass? _____

b. How was this achieved? _____

c. Where was the intended ultimate destination? _____

10. Describe response and fate of the powerful Ruler of the country they left behind. _____

My score is _____.   Well done!!!

(You might care to repeat this exercise at a later date to increase your score!)

How happy are the poor in spirit; theirs is the kingdom of heaven.
Happy are the gentle; they shall have the earth for their heritage.
Happy those who mourn; they shall be comforted.
Happy those who hunger and thirst for what is right; they shall be satisfied.
Happy the merciful; they shall have mercy shown them.
Happy the pure in heart; they shall see God.
Happy the peacemakers; they shall be called sons of God.
Happy those who are persecuted in the cause of right; theirs is the kingdom of heaven.
(The Sermon on the Mount: The Beatitudes.   Matthew 5:3)

(Answers overleaf.)

"The Exodus"

1. From which country did the Exodus take place? *Egypt*

2. What was the title of this country's ruler? *Pharoah*

3a. Who were the people emigrating? *The Israelites*

b. How did they come to be in this land in the first place? *Through Joseph having been sold into slavery; his brothers and family invited him during times of famine.*

c. Why did the Ruler resist their departing? *They were a significant part of his workforce; they had acquired valuable livestock*

4a. Name the leader or advocate for the people of the Exodus. *Moses*

b. This man was highly educated, which was unusual. How would this have occurred? *He was raised as a son of Pharaoh's daughter (privileged)*

c. Who was his older brother? *Aaron (Moses was 80 yrs ; brother 83 yrs)*

d. What was his brother's occupation? *Priest*

e. The brother carried a *rod/staff* when called upon to show God's might.

5. *"Let my people go that they may serve me."*
   But, the Ruler would not! **So -** plague after plague afflicted the country.

a. How many plagues were there? *Ten (10)*

b. The last was the most terrible. What was it? *Death of the firstborn of every person and animal*

6. Is anyone clever enough to name the 10 plagues in order? (Bonus 9 points)

1. *blood*	2. *frogs*	3. *lice*
4. *flies*	5. *disease of beasts*	6. *boils on man & beast*
7. *hails*	8. *locusts*	9. *darkness*
10. *death of firstborn*		

7. The plagues affected man and beast alike, the Exodus people being spared.

   What beasts / animals would have provided for the needs of the peoples of that land? *Cattle, horses, asses, camels, oxen, sheep, goats*

8. Think of any preparation for the Exodus the departing tribes were told to

   undertake. *Passover meal & sacrifice; baked cakes – unleavened due to haste; gathered herds ; 7 days of unleavened bread*

9a. Through which sea did the Exodus pass? *The Sea of Reeds*

b. How was this achieved? *Moses raised his staff and stretched out his hand over the sea which parted; they walked on dry land; the angel who lead stayed at their rear*

c. Where was the intended ultimate destination? *The promised land / land of milk & honey / land of the Canaanites*

10. Describe response and fate of the powerful Ruler of the country they left behind. *Army chariots bogged as they followed into the Sea of Reeds, drowned as Moses stretched his hand over the sea and waters returned.*

Did you ever wonder WHY?

Consider each of these and offer an explanation.   The reference will provide context.

(John 20:6…)

The cloth covering the head of the risen Christ was folded / wrapped and set to one side of the emptied linen shroud.

(Deuteronomy 34:5…)

So Moses the servant of the Lord died there in the land of Moab, according to the word of the Lord. And He buried him in the land of Moab.
No man ever knew where this grave was.

(Luke 4:23)

Ye will surely say unto me this proverb
'Physician, heal thyself … … … … … …..'

Think about the differences in lifespans of these groups.
These are very considerable.
Compare groups with each other and with modern day era.

a) Adam 930 years; Methusaleh 969 years; Noah 950 years
b) Shem 600 years; Shelah 433 years
c) Nahor 148 years; Abraham 175 years; Isaac 180 years; Joseph 110 years
d) The Apostle Luke 84 years

11 Faithful Apostles
Peter
John - The Evangelist
& James, His Brother
Andrew
Philip
Thomas
Bartholomew
Matthew
James – Son of
Alphaeus
Simon The Zealot
Jude – Son of James
(Thaddaeus)

The Apostle
James

Sometimes called St. James the Less

❖ Son of Alphaeus, first cousin of Jesus

❖ Head of Church at Jerusalem where called 'James the Just'

❖ Reconciled Jewish tradition with Christianity, thus a Christian Jew

❖ Won many converts to Christianity
SO

❖ Scribes and Pharisees plotted to kill him

❖ Martyred around 62 A.D.

❖ Said to have been thrown from the pinnacle of the Temple, then stoned and clubbed

***Blessings on him who comes
in the name of the Lord!***

WHO ARE THEY?

Sort out these jumbled names to identify the women that the bible (and indeed history) writes about. Simply rearrange the letters.

1. CLAPORATE	10. ABEEHILTZ ....
2. HURT	11. AH RAG ....
3. HEAL	12. THIDUJ ....
4. CHARLE	13. I MOAN ....
5. HORA BED	14. BELJEZE ....
6. HOARD	15. ASHAR ....
7. HARK BEE	16. DAILY ....
8. BHASE	17. AJ ANON ....
9. VEE	18. AIL HELD ....

'I am the handmaid of the Lord. Let what you have said be done to me.'
Luke 1:38

(Answers overleaf.)

Answers to 'WHO ARE THEY?'

1. CLAPORATE	*Cleopatra*	10. ABEEHILTZ	*Elizabeth*
2. HURT	*Ruth*	11. AH RAG	*Hagar*
3. HEAL	*Leah*	12. THIDUJ	*Judith*
4. CHARLE	*Rachel*	13. I MOAN	*Naomi*
5. HORA BED	*Deborah*	14. BELJEZE	*Jezebel*
6. HOARD	*Rhoda*	15. ASHAR	*Sarah*
7. HARK BEE	*Rebekah*	16. DAILY	*Lydia*
8. BHASE	*Sheba*	17. AJ ANON	*Joanna*
9. VEE	*Eve*	18. AIL HELD	*Delilah*

'For the moment your greeting reached my ears,

the child in my womb leapt for joy.'

Luke 1:44

KNOW YOUR NUMBERS

Read each phrase carefully and consider which numeral is its closest match.

Write your choice beside the phrase. Numbers may be used multiple times.

0; 1; 2; 3; 6; 7; 10; 11; 12; 20; 30; 40; 70; 900⁺

a) Pieces of silver paid as blood money to Judas

b) Years of Israelites' captivity in Babylon

c) Children of Abraham with Sarah

d) Days John the Baptist wandered in the wilderness

e) Plagues brought upon Pharaoh and Egypt

f) Sons of Jacob

g) Ministry years of Jesus

h) Days Jonah travelled with the whale

i) Commandments on the tablets of stone

j) Children of Uriah the Hittite

k) Numbers of times Peter denied knowing Jesus

l) Lifespan of Methuselah

m) Days of Creation in Genesis

n) Husbands of Ruth

o) Days of the Great Flood when Noah called the Ark home

p) Number of disciples following Judas's death

q) Number of disciples following Judas's death

r) Years Israelites wandered in the desert post-Exodus

s) Lifespan of Noah

t) Sons of Adam and Eve

My score is ___ / 20 .

(Answers overleaf.)

73

Answers to
KNOW YOUR NUMBERS

a) Pieces of silver paid as blood money to Judas — 30

b) Years of Israelites' captivity in Babylon — 70

c) Children of Abraham with Sarah (Isaac) — 1

d) Days John the Baptist wandered in the wilderness — 40

e) Plagues brought upon Pharaoh and Egypt — 7

f) Sons of Jacob — 12

g) Ministry years of Jesus — 3

h) Days Jonah travelled with the whale — 40

i) Commandments on the tablets of stone — 10

j) Children of Uriah the Hittite — 0 (wife then widow – Bathsheba)

k) Numbers of times Peter denied knowing Jesus — 3

l) Lifespan of Methuselah — 900+

m) Days of Creation in Genesis — 6 (The 7th day God rested.)

n) Husbands of Ruth — 2

o) Days of the Great Flood when Noah called the Ark home — 40

p) Number of disciples following Judas's death — 11

q) Times God called Samuel — 3

r) Years Israelites wandered in the desert post-Exodus — 40

s) Lifespan of Noah — 900+

t) Sons of Adam and Eve — 3 (Cain, Abel, Seth)

NOAH'S ARK NUMBER CHART

There are lots of lessons to learn from Noah. Think about the ones written here.
Then turn over the page to create your own.

one
We all share **one** Earth.   Look after it!

two
(by two)
Choose a good mate to travel with you in life.

three
When God speaks, listen.   He knows where you are going. You only think you do.

four
Remember that God called Noah – and Abraham – when they were advanced in years. It is never too late to be useful.

five
One Noah, one Ark! You too may have to do 'something big'. Like Noah, follow the plan. Take care of even the smallest details. Who can tell how many you will keep afloat?

six
Also remember faith gives you courage. So - resist detractors. They are unproductive. Custom build your own future!

seven
Don't go to bed without having done one positive thing. Each forward step you take helps keep your 'Ark' on course.

eight
Don't gauge your progress by where others are going. Maintain your objectives. Noah didn't drown!

nine
There was no 'champagne launching' of the Ark.
Neither did it sink!

ten
Whilst afloat in your 'Ark', relax, reflect, review and refresh. Are you ready for the next adventure?

eleven
Keep an eye to the horizons for high, dry ground. Pray that all of your efforts ensure a safe landing on your own 'Ararat'!

twelve
May your lives be swathed in rainbows.

NOAH'S ARK NUMBER CHART

Devise some lessons to share from Noah and his wonderful Ark.

Match your ideas to the numbers.

one _____

two
(*by two*) _____

three _____

four _____

five _____

six _____

seven _____

eight _____

nine _____

ten _____

eleven _____

twelve _____

'COUNT-DOWN' SONGS TO SING

THE TWELVE DAYS OF CHRISTMAS

On the <u>first</u> day of Christmas, my true love
sent to me: *a partridge in a pear tree*.
On the <u>second</u> day of Christmas, my true
love sent to me:
2 turtle doves and *a partridge in a pear tree*.
On the <u>third</u> day of Christmas, my true love
sent to me: *3 French hens*, *2 turtle doves*
and a partridge in a pear tree.
On the <u>fourth</u> day of Christmas, my true love
sent to me: *4 calling birds*, *3 French hens*,
2 turtle doves and a partridge in a pear tree.
On the <u>fifth</u> day of Christmas, my true love
sent to me: *5 gold rings*, *4 calling birds*,
3 French hens, *2 turtle doves*
and a partridge in a pear tree.
On the <u>sixth</u> day of Christmas, my true love
sent to me: *6 geese a-laying*, *5.. 4.. 3.. 2..*
and a partridge in a pear tree.
On the <u>seventh</u> day of Christmas, my true
love sent to me: *7 swans a-swimming*,
6 geese a-laying, *5.. 4.. 3.. 2..*
and a partridge in a pear tree.
On the <u>eighth</u> day of Christmas, my true love
sent to me: *8 maids a-milking*, *7..6..5..4..3..2*
and a partridge in a pear tree.
On the <u>ninth</u> day of Christmas, my true
love sent to me: *9 ladies leaping*, *8 maids*
a-milking, *7.. 6.. 5.. 4.. 3.. 2..*
and a partridge in a pear tree.
On the <u>tenth</u> day of Christmas, my true love
sent to me: *10 lords a-leaping*,
9.. 8.. 7.. 6.. 5.. 4.. 3.. 2..
and a partridge in a pear tree.
On the <u>eleventh</u> day of Christmas, my true
love sent to me:
11 pipers piping, *10..9..8..7..6..5..4..3..2..*
and a partridge in a pear tree.
On the <u>twelfth</u> day of Christmas, my true
love sent to me:
12 drummers drumming, *11 pipers piping*,
10 lords a- leaping, *9 ladies leaping*, *8 maids*
a-milking, *7 swans a-swimming*,
6 geese a-laying. *5 gold rings*, *4 calling birds*, *3*
French hens, *two turtle doves*
AND a partridge in a pear tree!

CHILDREN GO WHERE I SEND YOU
Words underlined start each verse, then follow pattern.
There are several versions of this gospel song.

<u>Children go where I send you.</u>
<u>How shall I send you?</u>
<u>I'm going to send you</u>

one by one. One for the little bitty baby;
was born, born, born in Bethlehem.

two by two. Two for Paul and Silas;
one for the little bitty baby; was born,
born, born in Bethlehem.

three by three. Three for the Hebrew
children; two for Paul and Silas;
one for the little bitty baby; was born,
born, born in Bethlehem.

(4 by 4) 4 for the poor that stood at the door

(5 by 5) 5 for the gospel preacher

(6 by 6) 6 for the 6 that couldn't get fixed

(7 by 7) 7 for the 7 that all went to heaven

(8 by 8) 8 for the 8 that stood at the gate

(9 by 9) 9 for the 9 that stood in the line

(10 by 10) 10 for the 10 commandments

(11 by 11) 11 for 11 of 'em singing in
heaven

(12 by 12) 12 for the 12 disciples;
        11 for 11 of 'em singing in heaven
        10 for the 10 commandments
        9 for the 9 that stood in the line
        8 for the 8 that stood at the gate
        7 for the 7 that all went to heaven
        6 for the 6 that couldn't get fixed
        5 for the gospel preacher
        4 for the poor that stood at the door
        3 for the Hebrew children
        2 for Paul and Silas;
one for the little bitty baby; was born, born,
        born in Bethlehem.

The Apostle
Bartholomew

❖ From Cana in Galilee

❖ Preached the Good News widely

❖ Thought to have converted the Armenian King

❖ Martyred at the hands of the Armenian King's brother in a manner of unspeakable cruelty

❖ Relics eventually transferred to Rome

'Here is my servant whom I have chosen,
My beloved, the favourite of my soul.
I will endow him with my spirit,
And he will proclaim the true faith to the
nations.
He will not brawl or shout,
Nor will anyone hear his voice on the streets.
He will not break the crushed reed,
nor put out the smouldering wick
till he has led the truth to victory:
In his name the nations will put their hope.'

Isaiah 42:1

Create your own

ALPHABET OF BIBLE PLACES

Match the names of any Old or New Testament places (towns, cities, countries, rivers, seas, mountains, areas . . .) with the alphabet. How many can you find / think of?

A _____ B _____

C _____ D _____

E _____ F _____

G _____ H _____

I _____ J _____

K _____ L _____

M _____ N _____

P _____ O _____

Q _____ R _____

S _____ T _____

U _____ V _____

W _____ X _____

Y _____ Z _____

I found _____ names of places in the Bible to match the letters!

CHECKLIST for ALPHABET OF BIBLE PLACES

A *Achaia, Alexandria, Arimathaea, Athens, Arabia, Asia, Assyria, Antioch, Ararat, Amphipolis, Apollonia*

B *Babel, Babylon, Bethlehem, Bethany, Bethel, Bethesda*

C *Caesaria, Calvary, Cana, Canaan, Cyrene, Capernaum, Cappadocia, Chaldea, Coos, Cilicia, Corinth, Cyprus, Chebar*

D *Derbe, Damascus, Decapolis*

E *Ephesus, Eden, Egypt, Elam, Earth*

F *Fuller's Field, (Firmament)*

G *Galatia, Gaza, Gall, Gethsemane, Golan, Golgotha, Gomorrah, Goshen, Greece, Galilee*

H *Hebron, Hades, Hell, Hierapolis, Heaven, Hazeroth*

I *Iconium, Israel, India, Italy*

J *Judaea, Jerusalem, Jericho, Jordan*

K *Kedron / Kidron, Kib'roth-hatta'avah*

L *Lystra, Libya, Laodicea, Lebanon, (Lake..)*

M *Macedonia, Mount of Olives, (Mounts ...), Mysia, Melita, Magdala, Memphis, Mars' Hill, Mesopotamia*

N *Neapolis, Nazareth, Nebo*

O *Olivet, Olympas*

P *Phrygia, Phoenicia, Palestine, Patara,' Pamphylia, Paradise, Pergamos, Persia, Philadelphia, Patmos*

Q

R *Rhodes, Red Sea, Rome, (Sea of Reeds)*

S *Sodom, Syria, Samothracia, Sidon, Salmone, Salem, Syracuse, Smyrna, Samaria, Sharon, Sheba, Shiloh*

T *Troas, Thyatira, Thessalonica, Tyre, Tel-a'bib, Tarsus*

U *Ulai, Ur*

V

W *(Wells), (Walls)*

X

Y

Z *Zion, Zidon*

(This list is not exhaustive but should get you going !)

HIDDEN PLACES

recorded in the Bible

28 place names are to be discovered within the words and across adjacent words in this story. Circle or underline each one you find and add each to the list you create in the column on the left.

. . . .
. . . .
. . . .
. . . .
. . . .
. . . .
. . . .
. . . .
. . . .
. . . .
. . . .
. . . .
. . . .
. . . .
. . . .
. . . .
. . . .
. . . .
. . . .
. . . .
. . . .
. . . .
. . . .
. . . .

Score:

/ 28

Gosh! Entry to this garden was an experience. Its red entry gate led to concreted pathways lined with interesting blue lamps. Gallons of water flowed through fountains encircled with shells. Definitely no retro aspects in sight!

Visitors were welcomed by the guides, Raj or Dan. No sale man with his glib yarns was tolerated.

With his helpers, a gardening guru laid down spring bulbs. These energetic 'stars' use only the best products. No ugly straw to be seen anywhere. As for the lawns, one wonders, 'Does he bale the cut long grass?'

On the far slopes, tyres were recycled to contain erosion. Raked Rondeletia beds concealed them. Roses of Sharon were the palest in each of the other beds which lined paths to a pergola then summer house. This had spectacular Corinthian columns and gates with chrome trims. It was also dome-shaped. High tea was served in fine bone china cups. Shades unfurled to keep out the hot sun. There was even a mango laneway to the lake.

One asks – can any visit to a garden be better?

(Answers overleaf.)

Answers to HIDDEN PLACES recorded in the Bible

Gosh! Entry to this garden was an experience. Its red entry gate led to concreted pathways lined with interesting blue lamps. Gallons of water flowed through fountains encircled with shells. Definitely no retro aspects in sight!

Visitors were welcomed by the guides, Raj or Dan. No sale man with his glib yarns was tolerated.

With his helpers, a gardening guru laid down spring bulbs. These energetic 'stars' use only the best products. No ugly straw to be seen anywhere. As for the lawns, one wonders, 'Does he bale the cut long grass?'

On the far slopes, tyres were recycled to contain erosion. Raked Rondeletia beds concealed them. Roses of Sharon were the palest in each of the other beds which lined paths to a pergola then summer house. This had spectacular Corinthian columns and gates with chrome trims. It was also dome-shaped. High tea was served in fine bone china cups. Shades unfurled to keep out the hot sun. There was even a mango laneway to the lake.

One asks – can any visit to a garden be better?

PLACES VISITED IN THE BIBLE

Can you name them?

Some places are hidden in anagrams, others need the missing letters to identify them.

1. THESE MANGE

_ _ _ _ _ _ _ _ _ _ _

2. MORE _ _ _ _ _

3. LEMON HIP

_ _ _ _ _ _ _ _ _

4. A A CHAI _ _ _ _ _ _

5. HA! GOT LOG

_ _ _ _ _ _ _ _

6. INCH ROT

_ _ _ _ _ _ _

7. C TREE _ _ _ _ _ _

8. AS MARIA

_ _ _ _ _ _ _

9. IS LOVE

(Mount of) _ _ _ _ _ _

10. LOOSE SAC

_ _ _ _ _ _ _ _ _

11. NEED _ _ _ _

12. GALA DAM

_ _ _ _ _ _ _

13. M _ _ _ D _ _ I A

14. _ A L _ _ R Y

15. _ A L _ _ E E

16. C I L _ _ I A

17. E _ H _ S U _

18. A _ A _ _ T

19. _ Y R _ _ E

20. J _ _ _ A N

21. J U _ _ E _

22. _ E T _ _ N Y

23. _ E _ H _ E _ E _

24. RULE JAMES

_ _ _ _ _ _ _ _ _

25. R Y T E _ _ _ _

26. THEN ZARA

_ _ _ _ _ _ _ _

Score: ... / 26

(Answers overleaf.)

PLACES VISITED IN THE BIBLE

1. THESE MANGE

   Gethsemane

2. MORE *Rome*

3. LEMON HIP

   Philemon

4. A ACHAI *Achaia*

5. HA! GOT LOG

   Golgotha

6. INCH ROT

   Corinth

7. C TREE *Crete*

8. AS MARIA

   Samaria

9. IS LOVE

   (Mount of) *Olives*

10. LOOSE SAC

    Colossae

11. N E E D *Eden*

12. GALA DAM

    Magdala

13. M *ACE* DON I A

14. *C* A L *VAR* Y

15. *GA* L *IL* E E

16. C I L *IC* I A

17. E *P* H *E* S U *S*

18. A *R* A R *A* T

19. *C* Y R *E N* E

20. J *OR D* A N

21. J *UD* A E *A*

22. *B* E T *HA* N Y

23. *B* E T H L *E* H *E M*

24. R U L E J A M E S

    J E R U S A L E M

25. R Y T E *Tyre*

26. T H E N Z A R A

    N A Z A R E T H

    Score: . . . / 26

HIDDEN BOOKS OF THE OLD TESTAMENT

There are 19 hidden books of the Old Testament in this grid, both horizontally and vertically orientated, forwards and backwards, downwards and upwards. One occurs twice. Draw a line through each one you find and write its name in the space provided below. You will discover that 25 extra letters fill the gaps remaining. Write these in the order they appear starting with the top row from left to right.

The Secret Message is one that should never be kept secret!

A	U	H	S	O	J	L	M	I	P
M	A	L	A	C	H	I	I	S	S
O	O	A	V	E	T	H	C	A	A
S	A	M	U	E	L	Y	A	I	L
N	E	E	I	Z	G	R	H	A	M
D	A	N	I	E	L	U	M	H	S
H	H	T	B	K	O	T	A	S	S
O	B	A	D	I	A	H	L	R	I
S	U	T	R	E	Z	R	A	E	S
E	A	I	S	L	T	H	C	B	E
A	J	O	N	A	H	Y	H	M	N
S	E	N	A	H	U	M	I	U	E
L	F	S	O	L	O	M	O	N	G

Horizontal   1 . . . .   2 . . . .   3 . . . .   4 . . . .

5 . . . .   6 . . . .   7 . . . .   8 . . . .   9 . . . .

Vertical   1 . . . .   2 . . . .   3 . . . .   4 . . . .

5 . . . .   6 . . . .   7 . . . .   8 . . . .   9 . . . .

10 . . . .   11 . . . .   My score is _____ / 20

Secret Message: _ _ _ _   _ _ _   _ _ _ _ _ _   _ _ _ _ _ _ _ _   _ _ _ _ _ _   _ _ _ _ _ .

85

HIDDEN BOOKS OF THE OLD TESTAMENT

A	U	H	S	O	J	L	M	I	P
M	A	L	A	C	H	I		S	S
O	O	A	V	E	T	H	C	A	A
S	A	M	U	E	L	Y	A	I	L
N	E	E	I	Z	G	R	H	A	M
D	A	N	I	E	L	U	M	H	S
H	H	T	B	K	O	T	A	S	S
O	B	A	D	I	A	H	L	R	I
S	U	T	R	E	Z	R	A	E	S
E	A		S	L	T	H	C	B	E
A	J	O	N	A	H	Y	H	M	N
S	E	N	A	H	U	M	I	U	E
L	F	S	O	L	O	M	O	N	G

Horizontal	1. *Joshua*	2. *Malachi*	3. *Samuel*	4. *Daniel*
5. *Obadiah*	6. *Ezra*	7. *Jonah*	8. *Nahum*	9 . *Solomon*

Vertical	1. *Amos*	2. *Hosea*	3. *Lamentations*	4. *Ezekiel*
5. *Ruth*	6. *Micah*	7. *Malachi*	8. *Isaiah*	9. Numbers
10. *Psalms*	11. *Genesis*			**My score is** _____ / 20

Secret Message: *L O V E   T H Y   N E I G H B O U R   A S   T H Y S E L F.*

11 Faithful Apostles

Peter

John - The Evangelist

& James, His Brother

Andrew

Philip

Thomas

Bartholomew

Matthew

James – Son of

Alphaeus

Simon The Zealot

Jude – Son of James
(Thaddaeus)

The Apostle
Matthew

❖ Also known as Levi, son of Alphaeus

❖ Born Capernaum

❖ Tax collector and thus initially despised for this

❖ Rose to the dignity of loyal, dedicated, talented disciple

❖ Credited with writing the First Gospel (in Aramaic)

❖ Carried the Good News to Persia and Ethiopia

❖ Faithful to his Jewish traditions

❖ Martyred in Ethiopia

❖ Pope Gregory VII records that his relics were transferred to Salerno in the tenth century

I am the gate.
Anyone who enters through me will be safe:
He will go freely in and out
And be sure of finding pasture.
John 10:9

The Apostle
Jude

❖ Patron Saint of Hopeless Causes / Impossible Cases

❖ Known as Jude (or Lebbaeus) Thaddeus

❖ Son of James

❖ Preached the Good News in Egypt, Mauritania and Persia

❖ Believed to have been martyred by crucifixion in Persia, where he had travelled with Simon

'Not even the Archangel Michael, when he was engaged in argument with the devil about the corpse of Moses, dared to denounce him in the language of abuse. All he said was, "Let the Lord correct you". But these people abuse anything they do not understand; and, the only things they do understand - just by nature like unreasoning animals - will turn out to be fatal to them.'

Jude 1: 9,10

11 Faithful Apostles

Peter

John - The Evangelist

& James, His Brother

Andrew

Philip

Thomas

Bartholomew

Matthew

James – Son of

Alphaeus

Simon The Zealot

Jude – Son of James
(Thaddaeus)

Tribes, Wives & A Dream !

Answers overleaf.

TRIBES

Complete these. Details of the tribes of Israel are to be found in Genesis.
(From Chapter 29 on.)

1. How many tribes of Israel were there? _____

2. 'Israel' was the new name given to which man? _____

3. The tribes descended from Israel's sons.

    a) Who was the oldest son? _____

    b) Name the youngest. _____

    c) Which one was kidnapped and sold? _____

4. Describe the garment Israel had made for him. _____
    _____

5. Name any of the other sons of Israel. _____
    _____

6. Israel's sons were born of 2 wives and 2 servants.

    a) Who was the first wife?   _____

    b) Which wife was the most loved?   _____

    c) Which wife died in childbirth? _____

    d) How many sons did she have? _____

7. To which country did the tribes move for 430 years? _____

SCORE: _ _ _ /20

WIVES

Whose wife is she?

1. Rebekkah _____

2. Herodias _____

3. Bathsheba _____

4. Eve _____

5. Sarah (Sarai) _____

6. Leah _____

7. Elizabeth _____

8. Hagar _____

9. Zipporah _____

10. Ruth _____

11. Abigail _____

12. Asenath _____

SCORE: _ _ / 15

DREAM

(Genesis 28:12; 35:15)
"And he dreamed, and behold a ladder set up on the earth, and the top of it reached to Heaven, and behold the angels of God ascending and descending on it . . ."

a) To whom was this dream sent?

_ _ _ _ _ _ _ _ _ _

b) What was the promise God revealed in it?

_ _

_ _

c) The site was marked with a stone pillar and called _ _ _ _ _ _ _ _ _ _ _ _ _ _ _ _ _

At the time, the place was known as 'Luz'

ANSWERS TO Tribes:

1. 12
2. Jacob
3. a) Reuben b) Benjamin
   c) Joseph;
4. a coat of many colours
5. In order: Reuben Simeon,
   Levi, Judah, Dan,
   Naphtali, Gad, Asher,
   Issachar, Zebulun, Joseph,
   Benjamin
6. a) Leah   b) Rachel
   c) Rachel; d) 2 sons
7. Egypt

ANSWERS TO Wives

1. Rebekkah to Isaac
2. Herodias to Herod
3. Bathsheba to Uriah then
   David
4. Eve to Adam
5. Sarah (Sarai) to Abraham
6. Leah to Jacob
7. Elizabeth to Zacharias
8. Hagar (servant) to Abraham
9. Zipporah to Moses
10. Ruth (widow Naomi's son)
    then Boaz
11. Abigail to Nabal then
    David
12. Asenath to Joseph

& A Dream !

a) Jacob
b) God confirms his promise
   (as to Abraham) re
   descendants multiplying
   and spreading;
   and promises to be with
   him wherever he goes
c) Bethel

GENEALOGY OF THE TRIBES OF ISRAEL

FATHER	SPOUSE	CHILD
Abraham #	Sarah Wife	Isaac #
	Hagar Servant	Ishmael
Isaac #	Rebekkah Wife	Esau; Jacob (Israel) #
Jacob # called 'Israel'	Leah Wife	1. Reuben 2. Simeon 3. Levi 4. Judah 5. Issachar 6. Zebulun Dinah, daughter
	Zilpah Leah's Servant	1. Gad; 2. Asher
	Bilhah Rachel's servant	3. Dan; 4. Naphtali
	Rachel Wife	5. Joseph #; 6. Benjamin

90

11 Faithful Apostles	# The new 12ᵗʰ Apostle

11 Faithful Apostles

Peter

John - The Evangelist

& James, His Brother

Andrew

Philip

Thomas

Bartholomew

Matthew

James – Son of

Alphaeus

Simon The Zealot

Jude – Son of James
(Thaddaeus)

The new 12ᵗʰ Apostle
Matthias

❖ Chosen by the casting of lots amongst disciples

❖ Became the 12ᵗʰ Apostle after the Resurrection of Christ

❖ Replaced Judas Iscariot who had betrayed Jesus for 30 pieces of silver

❖ Had been in the company of Jesus and His disciples from the time of John the Baptist

❖ Preached the Good News to Cappadocia and precincts of the Caspian Sea

❖ Believed to have been martyred by crucifixion or beheading

❖ Relics said to have been transferred from Jerusalem to Rome

To love is to live according to His commandments: this is the commandment which you have heard since the beginning, to live a life of love.

2 John 1:16

Match and Mismatch

Circle or underline the 'mismatch' in each group. Justify your choice.

1) Reuben   Levi   Issachar   Gad   Dinah

2) Philip   Paul   Bartholomew   Thomas   Jude

3) Cain   Shem   Ham   Japheth

4) frogs   lice   mosquitoes   flies   locusts

5) Saul   David   Herod   Solomon   Judah

6) Seth   Methuselah   Abel   Cain

7) Aaron   Isaiah   Belshazzar   Daniel   Ezekiel

8) Uriah   Goliath   Potiphar   Malachi   Joshua

9) Annas   Caiaphas   Aaron   Abel

10)   Dan   Naphtali   Benjamin   Zebulon   Asher

11)   Cana   Nebo   Ararat   Moriah

12)   Galatians   Ephesians   Lamentations   Corinthians

13)   Nebuchanezzar   Shadrach   Meshach   Abednego   Daniel

14)   Jude   Joshua   Judges   Job   Jeremiah

15)   Arimathaea   Bethlehem   Emmaus   Ephraim   Damascus

Was there more than one possible answer?
My score is _____ **/ 15**
Answers page 90.

The Dreamers

Who dreamed the dream?
Write the dreamer's name on the line.

I. The image's head was of fine gold, his breast and arms of silver, his belly and thighs brass; his legs of iron and part of clay.

_____

II. And he dreamed, and behold a ladder set upon the earth, and the top of it reached to heaven . . . .

_____

III. In Gibeon, the Lord appeared to _____ in a dream by night: and God said, Ask what I shall give thee . . . Give therefore thy servant an understanding heart to judge thy people . . .

IV. Behold, the angel of the Lord appeared to him in a dream, saying, _____ , fear not to take unto thee . . . for thy wife: for that which is conceived in her . . . .

V. And being warned by God in a dream that they should not return to Herod, they departed into their own country another way.

_____

VI. When he was set down on the judgment seat, his wife sent to him saying, Have thou nothing to do with this just man: for I have suffered many things this day in a dream because of him.

_____ This was the wife of _____

VII. And, behold, there came up out of the river seven well-favoured kine and fat-fleshed; and they fed in the meadow. And, behold, seven other kine came up after them out of the river, ill-favoured and lean-fleshed . . . and the ill-favoured and lean-fleshed did eat up the seven well-favoured and fat kine . . .

_____

Score: _____ / 7

(Answers next page)

Answers to **The Dreamers**	Answers to **Match and Mismatch** (or accept reasonable explanation)
I. Nebuchanezzar (Daniel 2:31)	1. Gad; not a child of Leah **OR** Dinah only daughter (of Jacob)
II. Jacob (Genesis 28:12)	2. Paul; apostle but not one of 12 disciples
III. Solomon (1Kings 3:5)	3. Cain; son of Adam; others sons of Noah
IV. Joseph (Mary's betrothed) (Matthew 1:20)	4. mosquitoes; not one of the plagues of Egypt as were others
V. The 3 Wise men (Matthew 2:12)	5. Judah; not a king
VI. Wife of Pilate (Matthew 27:19)	6. Methusaleh: not a child of Adam and Eve
VII. Pharaoh (Genesis 41:5)	7. Belshazzar: not a prophet
	8. Malachi; not a soldier
	9. Abel; not a priest
	10. Benjamin; son of Rachel, others sons of slaves / maidservants
	11. Cana; not a mountain
	12. Lamentations; only one Old Testament or not letter of Paul
	13. Nebuchanezzar; a king, others were wise men / Hebrews
	14. Jude; only disciple / only New Testament Book

P
A
U
L

"The Apostle to the Gentiles"

- formerly 'Saul' of Tarsus
- tentmaker
- learned Pharisee
- dedicated to Judaic tradition
- mercilessly persecuted early Christians (Church of God)
- (Acts 9:1-19) converted by the Resurrected Jesus on the road to Damascus
- chosen by God to preach to pagans (the 'uncircumcised')
- travelled and preached widely (Corinth, Palestine, Macedonia, Ephesus, Arabia..)
- wrote his encouraging and instructional letters to Christian communities from approximately A.D. 45 onwards
- stoned, beaten, imprisoned (Rome)
- martyred by beheading around A.D. 67, near the site of the basilica in Rome

Angels

Messengers
Heavenly Hosts
Holy Myriads
Visible & Invisible
Agents of God's Will

Angels reveal their purpose

but rarely their names.

Hierarchies, ***Spheres*** *or* ***Choirs*** *of Angels have been suggested as possible, especially in Medieval theology. Several interesting variations exist from writings of:-*
1st century Clement of Rome;
4th century St Ambrose and St Jerome;
5th century Pseudo-Dionysius the Areopagite
6th century St Gregory the Great;
7th century St Isidore of Seville;
8th century John of Damascus;
11-12th century St Hildegard of Birgen;
13th century Thomas Aquinas;
14th century Dante Alighieri.

For example :-
1. Seraphim (*'burning ones'*) Isaiah 6:1-8
2. Cherubim Genesis 3:24; Ezekiel 10:12-14, 28: 14-16, Exodus 25:17-22, 1Kings 6:23-28 Revelation 4:6-8; 2Chronicles 3:7-14
3. Thrones (*or Elders*) Coloss. 1:16; Ezek.10:17
4. Dominions or Lordships
5. Virtues or Strongholds
6. Powers or Strongholds
7. Principalities or Rulers
8. Archangels ('chief angels') 1 Thess.4:16; Jude 1:9
9. Angels with Guardian Angels

What tasks allotted to angels are revealed in scripture?

Check the reference & describe the event.

Can you identify the angel? (Name? Choir?)

1. **Jacob & angel**   Genesis 32:29

2. **Joshua & angel**   Joshua 5:14

3. **Parents of Samson**   Judges 13:3-6; 9-22

4. **Apostle John**   Revelation 19:10; 22:8-9

5. **Angel & Satan**   Jude 8-10

In what context are these 'named' angels?

❖ **Michael**

❖ **Raphael** (Book of Tobit/Tobias not included in all versions of Bible)

❖ **Gabriel**

❖ **Uriel** (refer Book of Ezra)

The Archangel Raphael says he is 1 of 7 standing before the Lord.
What might this mean?

Which one is 'Prince of the army of Jehovah?

Some angels were 'lost' or 'fallen'.

Why did this occur?

Are there consequences?

Name Changers

You are going to 'morph' or change the top word into the bottom word. Do this by changing one letter at a time for each step, rearranging letters as necessary to create a new word for each step of the transition. There is more than one pathway to follow. Try to economise on the number of steps you take. Work upwards or downwards. *Example*: MARY to RUTH (MARY; **T**RAM; **H**ART; R**U**TH)

MARK - - - - - - - - - - - - LUKE	LUKE - - - - - - - - - - - - JOHN
MARK - - - - - - - - - - - - JOHN	JOHN - - - - - - - - - - - - PAUL
MARK - - - - - - - - - - - - PAUL	LUKE - - - - - - - - - - - - PAUL

GIFTS OF THE HOLY SPIRIT

All gifts from the Spirit combine for common good. They are allocated as the Spirit determines.

1 Corinthians 12

There are 9 gifts.

- ❖ Message of Wisdom
- ❖ Message of Knowledge
- ❖ Faith
- ❖ Gift of Healing
- ❖ Gift of Miraculous Power
- ❖ Prophesy
- ❖ Distinguishing Between Spirits
- ❖ Speaking in Different Kinds of Tongues
- ❖ Interpreting What Was Said in Tongues

Find examples of gifts of the Spirit in the Old Testament Books.

- - - - - - - - - - - - - - - - - - - -

- - - - - - - - - - - - - - - - - - - -

- - - - - - - - - - - - - - - - - - - -

What do these feasts commemorate?
4 FEASTS

1. The Passover
Exodus 12:1....; Leviticus 23:5

2. Unleavened Bread
Exodus 12:15; 23:15

3. First Fruits
Exodus 23:16; Leviticus 23:10

4. Pentecost
Leviticus 23:15; Acts 2:1,12

Pentecost falls 50 days (7 sabbaths) after First Fruits. It also marks the beginning of the church. At the celebration of Pentecost, the Holy Spirit descended upon the 11 faithful apostles and Matthias
Acts 2: 1-12
List signs of the Spirit's presence then:

- o
- o
- o
- o
- o

The Apostles were then heard to speak in such languages as ...

Revelation (Apocalyptic)

The Last Book

- Author John the Evangelist, son of Zebedee
- Received in a vision
- Dated probably in the 90s (AD)

4 theories concerning this book

(proposed at different stages)

- 1st : Preterist. This views the prophesies as being fulfilled in the early history of the Christian church; a period of persecution by the Roman Emperor (and others)
- 2nd: Historical. This portrays the history of the church from the days of John till the end of time
- 3rd: Idealist. This interprets the visions as an unfolding of great principles during relentless conflict, with no actual events
- 4th: Futurist. This seeks to interpret the text

The Last Antichrist

- Receives a head wound (perhaps by sword); would have been fatal but impossibly and astonishingly healed
- Performs great and miraculous signs, e.g. fire falling from heaven
- Forced worship of the beast on all
- Forced all to receive the mark of the beast on right hand or forehead. No buying or selling without this mark
- The mark is the beast's name or the number of his name. It is the number of a man, the number 666. This is not obvious.
- 'If anyone has insight (or understanding), let him calculate the number of the beast . . . .'

Significant numbers in Revelation:

3:- 3 angels; 3 plagues of fire, smoke and sulfur

4:- 4 living creatures; 4 horses- white, fiery red, black, pale; 4 angels

7:- 7 churches in Asia; 7 candlesticks; the book with 7 seals; 7 angels; 7 trumpets; 7 thunders; 7 plagues; 7 bowls of God's wrath; 7 horns and 7 eyes; 7 heads; 7 crowns; 7 spirits; 7 hills; 7 kings

10:- horns

12:- stars on a crown

24:-   elders   **42**:- months

666:- mark of the beast

1,000 ;- years Satan is bound;
              years Christ rules the earth

1,260:- days of prophesy; days of safe haven in desert for the woman and child, **144** cubits thick & **12,000** furlongs length, width, height

144,000:- 12,000 'sealed' servants of God from each of the tribes of Israel

200,000,000:- mounted troops

Signs and Portents

Earthquakes & conflict here & there
Blood-red moon and dark sun
False religion will spread over the earth
Global leader with global monetary system
Men will flee to caves in the rocks &
holes in the ground. (Isaiah 2)
People will be lovers of themselves, lovers of money; boastful, proud, abusive; disobedient to their parents; ungrateful, unholy, without love; unforgiving, slanderous, without self-control, brutal; not lovers of the good; treacherous, rash, conceited; lovers of pleasure rather than lovers of God . . . Have nothing to do with them.
(2 Timothy 3:1)
In the later days, some will abandon the faith and follow deceiving spirits and things taught by spirits . . . They forbid people to marry and order them to abstain from certain foods which God created to be received with thanksgiving . . . for everything God created is good . .
(1Timothy 4:1)

***ONLY** the **Father** knows the day and the time.*
***ANYONE** who calls on the name of the Lord will be saved (Joel 2:28)*

Where on Earth?

PART 1: 'Abraham's Era'   *Enter place names in the column beside their matching letter on the map.*

The Great Sea (a)

(Mediterranean Sea)

Black Sea (b)

Caspian Sea (c)

Persian Gulf (d)

Red Sea (e)

Aegean Sea (f)

Troy (g)

Caphtor (Crete) (h)

Kittim (Cyprus) (i)

Aleppo (j)

Ninevah (k)

Byblos (l)

Damascus (m)

Bethel (n)

Beersheba (o)

Noth (Memphis) (p)

Babylon (q)

Ur (r) Nile River (s)

Euphrates River (t)

Tigress River (u)

Position of Jordan River (v)

Sinai (w) Mt Ararat (x)

Hebron (y)

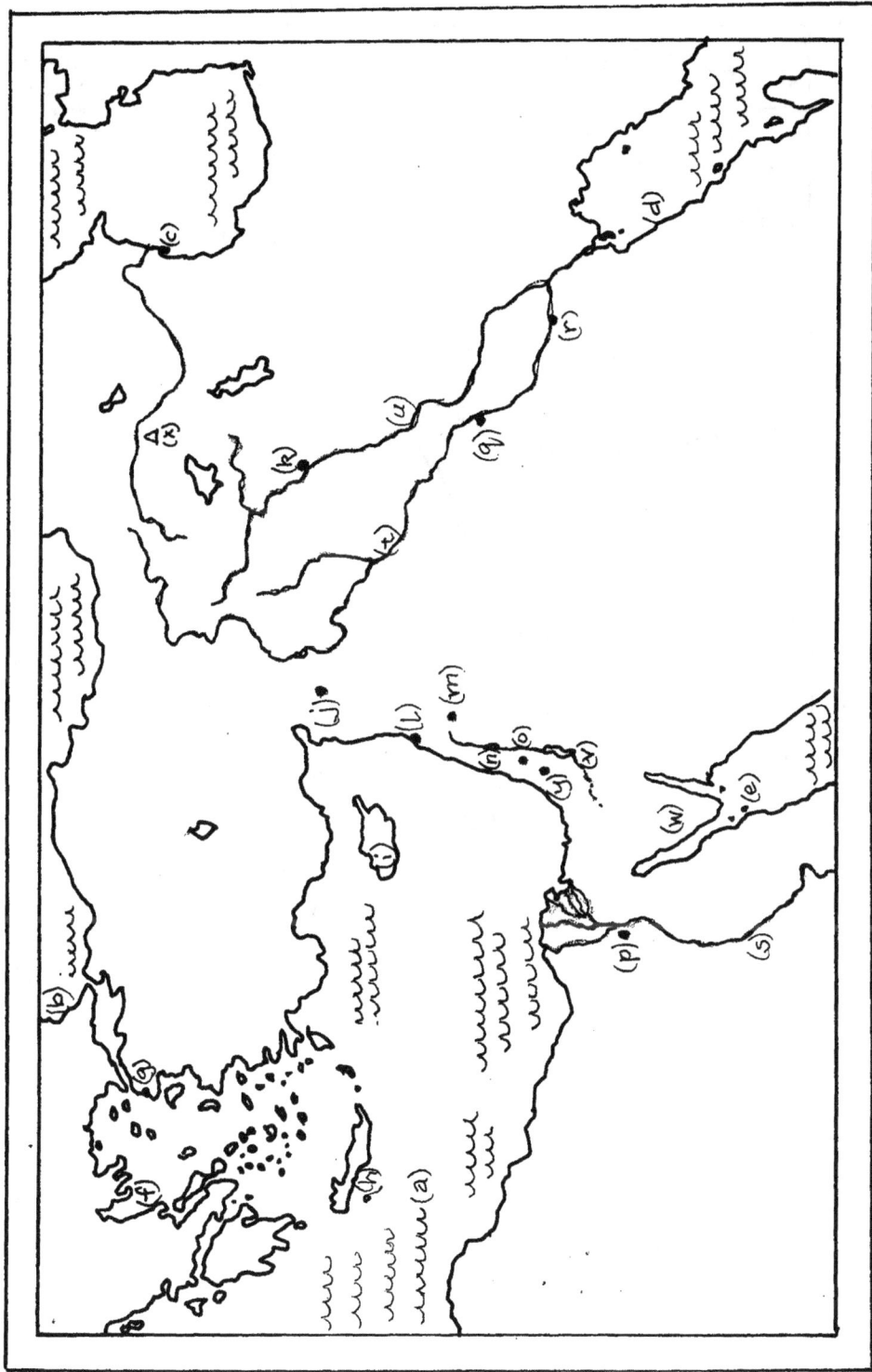

Part 1 (cont'd): *Now match the rearranged places in the column with letters on the map.*

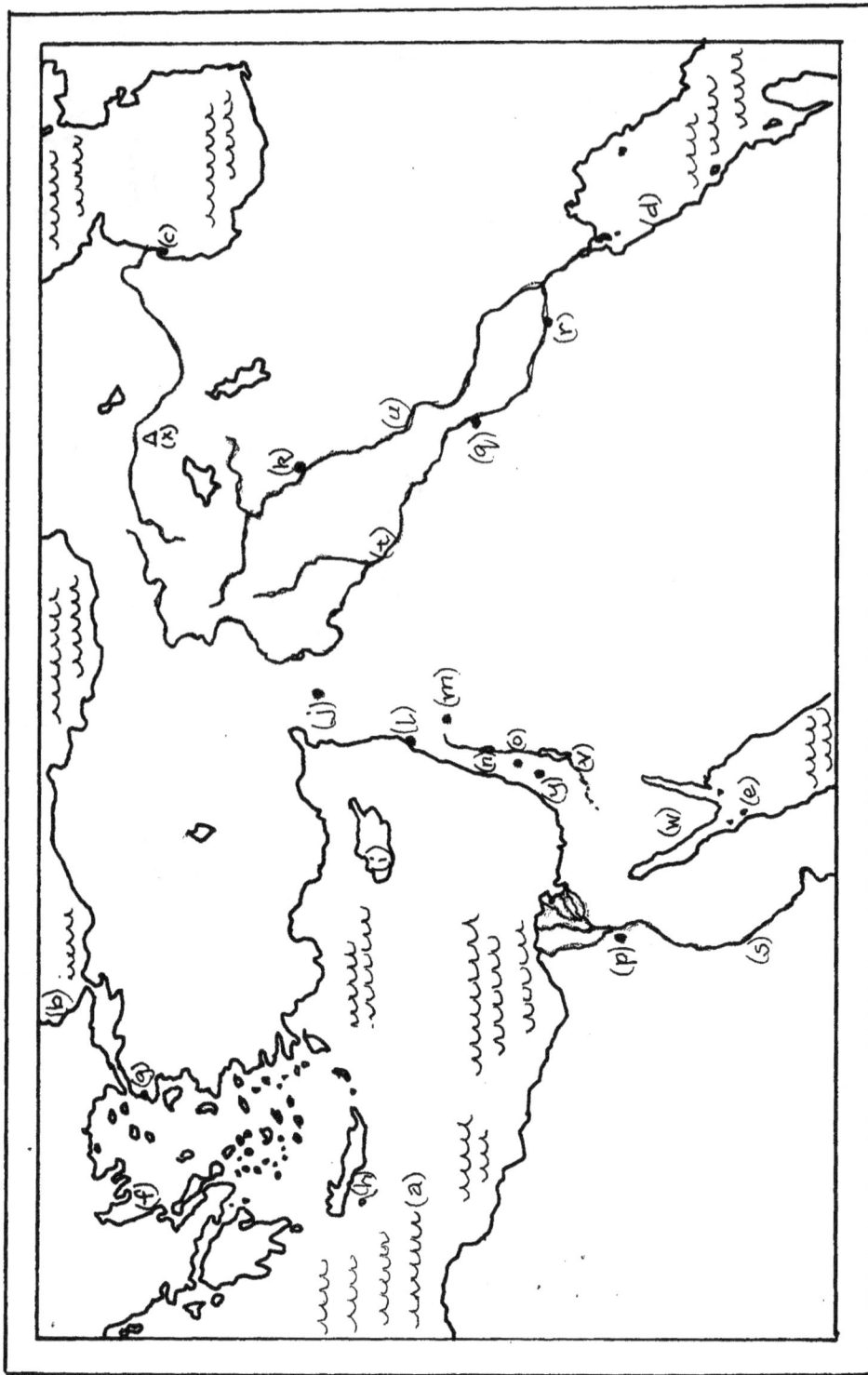

Place Names

Aegean Sea

Aleppo

Babylon

Beersheba

Bethel

*Black Sea

Byblos

Caphtor (Crete)

Caspian Sea

Damascus

Euphrates River

Hebron

Kittim (Cyprus)

Mt. Ararat

Nile River

Ninevah

Noth (Memphis)

Persian Gulf

Position of Jordan River

Red Sea; & * Sinai

The Great Sea (now

Mediterranean Sea)

Tigress River

Troy; & *Ur

Score: ..../ 25

Part 2: Era of Exodus

Enter the place names in the column beside their matching letter on the map.

Where on Earth?

The Great Sea (a)

Red Sea (b)

Salt Sea (c)

Sea of Kinnereth (d)

Jordan River (e)

Sinai (f)

Egypt (g)

Rameses (h)

Succoth (i)

Mt. Sinai (j)

Beersheba (k)

Hebron (l)

Jerusalem (m)

Jericho (n)

Bethel (o)

Nile River (p)

Noph (Memphis) (q)

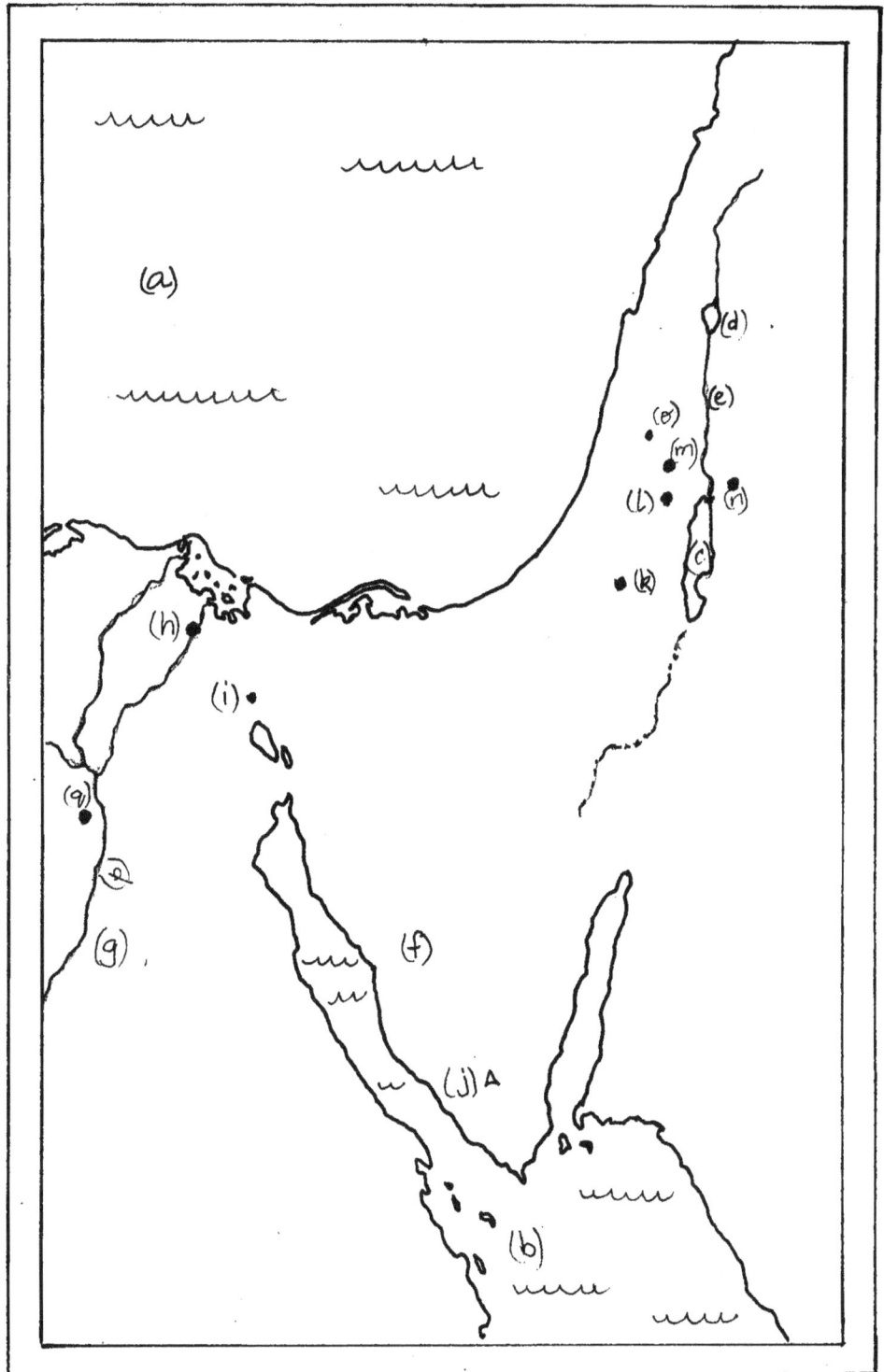

Part 2 (cont'd)

Now match the place names in the column with the letters on the map.

Place Names

Beersheba

Bethel

Egypt

Hebron

Jericho

Jerusalem

Jordan River

Mt. Sinai

Nile River

Noph (Memphis)

Rameses

Red Sea

Salt Sea

Sea of Kinnereth

Sinai

Succoth

The Great Sea

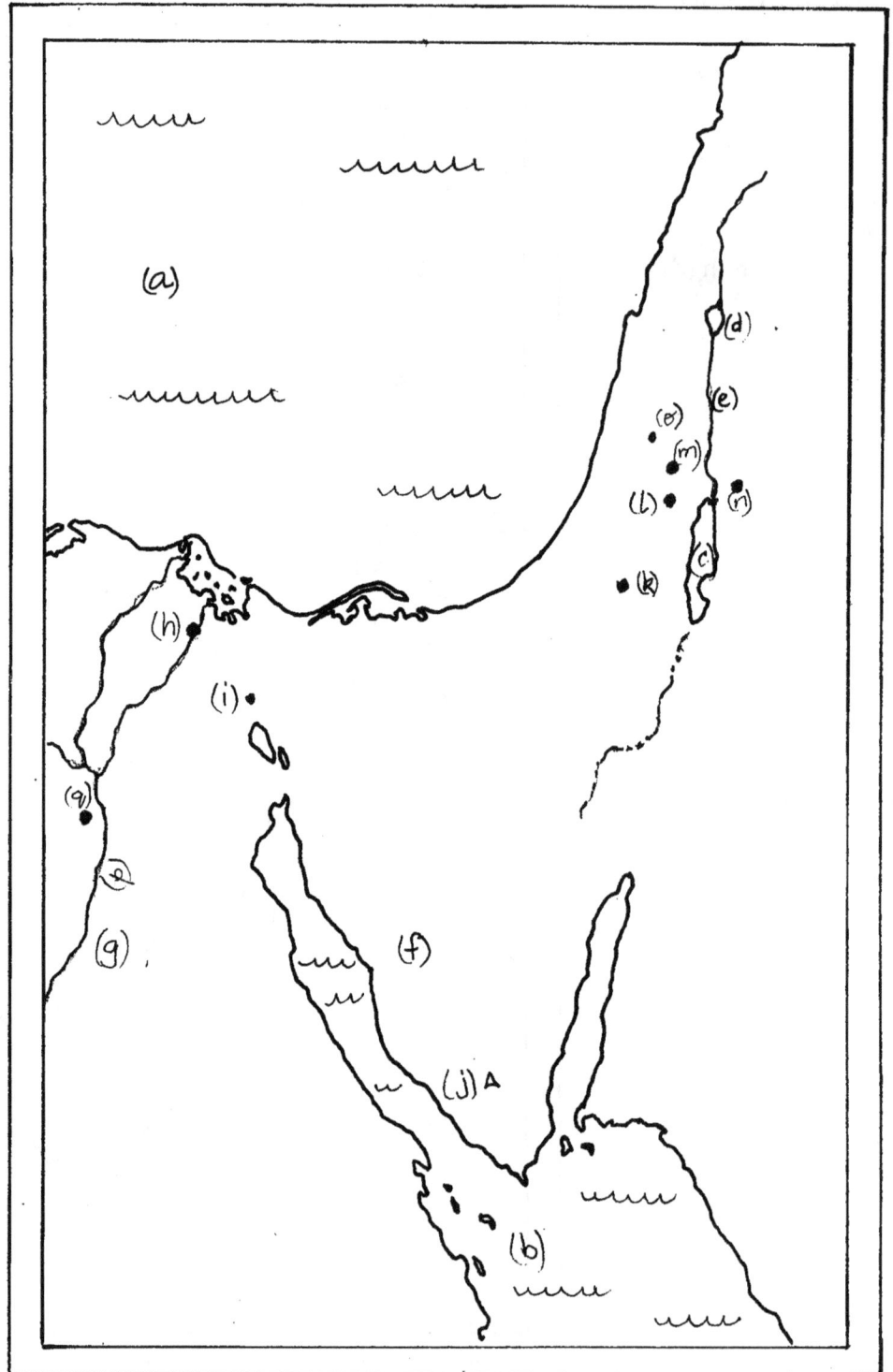

Score: ... / 17

Where on Earth? Part 3: Land of 12 Tribes of Israel

Enter each place name in the column beside its matching letter on the map.

Where on earth?

The Great Sea (a)

Gaza (b)

Joppa (c)

Beersheba (d)

Bethlehem (e)

Jerusalem (f)

Bethel (g)

Jericho (h)

Samaria (i)

Tyre (j)

Golan (k)

Dan (l)

Damascus (m)

Salt Sea (n)

Sea of Kinnereth (o)

Jordan River (p)

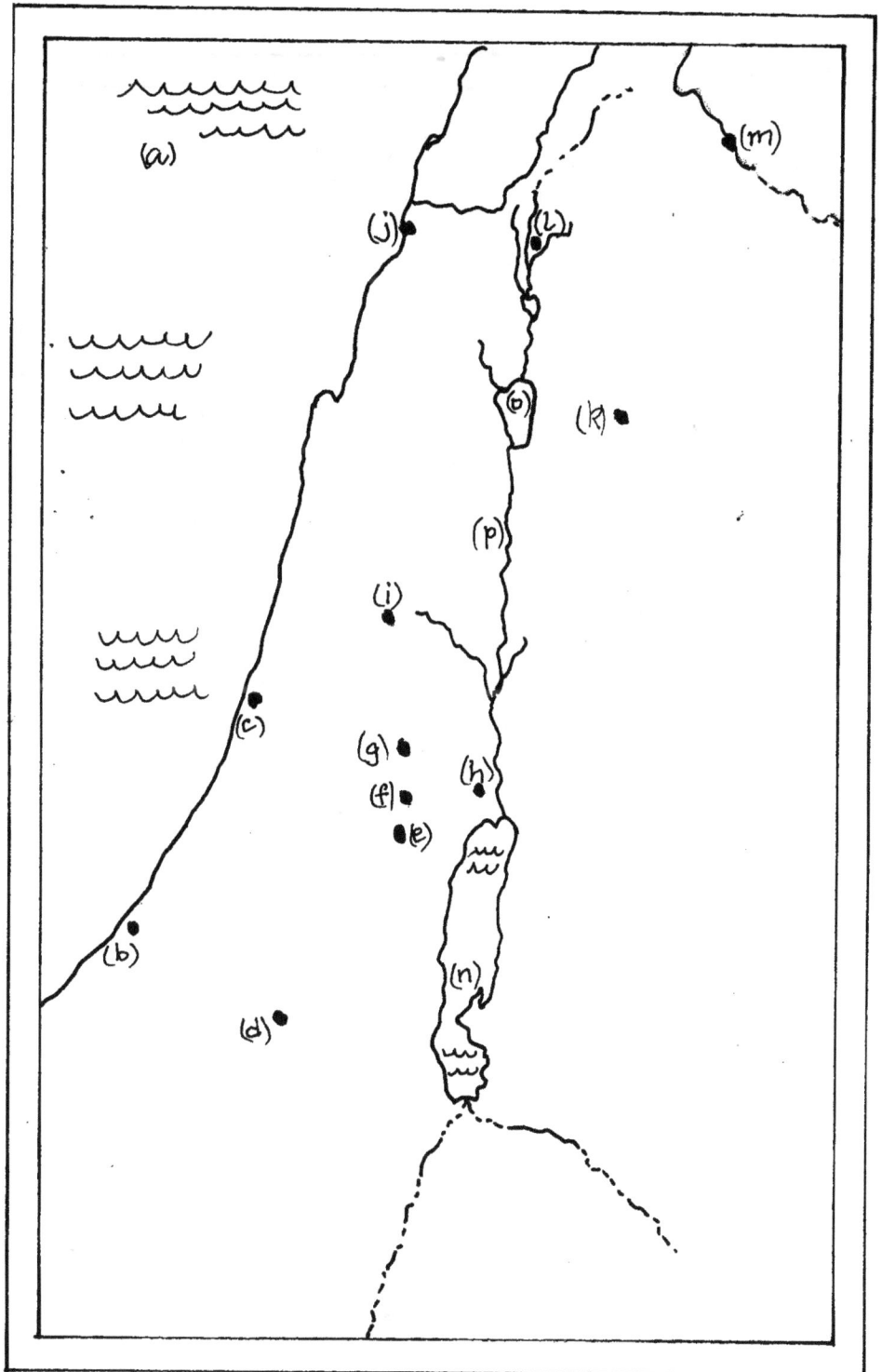

Where on Earth? Part 3: (cont'd)

Now match the rearranged place names in the column with the letters on the map.

PlaceNames

Beersheba

Bethel

Bethlehem

Damascus

Dan

Gaza

Golan

Jericho

Jerusalem

Joppa

JordanRiver

SaltSea

Samaria

SeaofKinnereth

TheGreatSea

Tyre

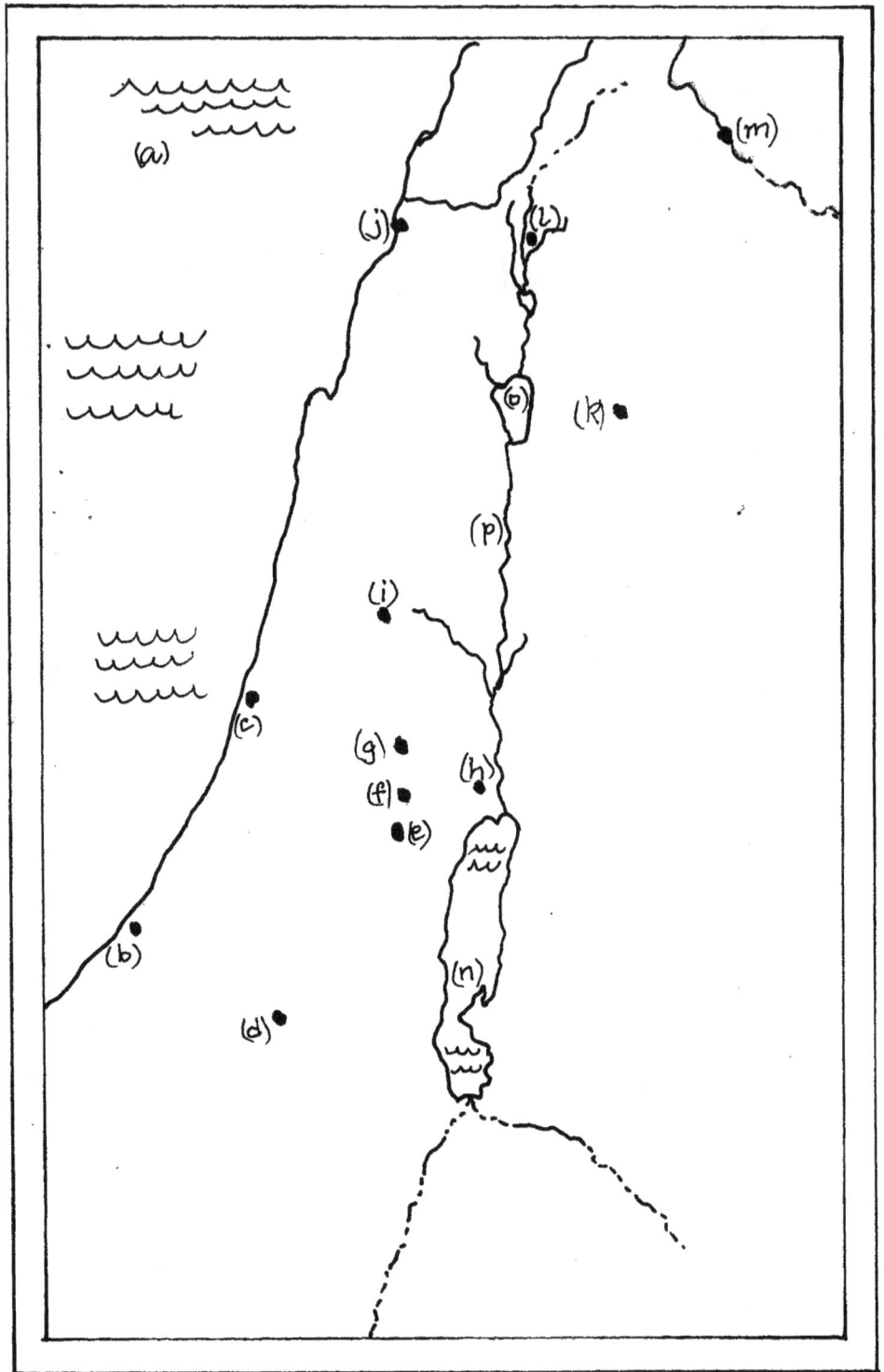

Total Score: ...... / 16

Where on Earth? Part 4: Kingdoms of David & Solomon

Enter each place name in the column beside its matching letter on the map.

Where on Earth?

Part 4

The Great Sea   (a)

Gulf of Aqaba   (b)

Salt Sea

(= *Dead Sea*)   (c)

Sea of Kinnereth

(= *Sea of Galilee*) (d)

Jordan River   (e)

Euphrates River (f)

Kittim

(= *Cyprus*)   (g)

Aleppo   (h)

Kadesh   (i)

Damascus   (j)

Sidon   (k)

Tyre   (l)

Joppa   (m)

Gaza   (n)

Gezer   (o)

Jerusalem   (p)

Hebron   (q)

Beersheba   (r)

Sinai   (s)

Tamar   (t)

Wadi of Egypt   (u)

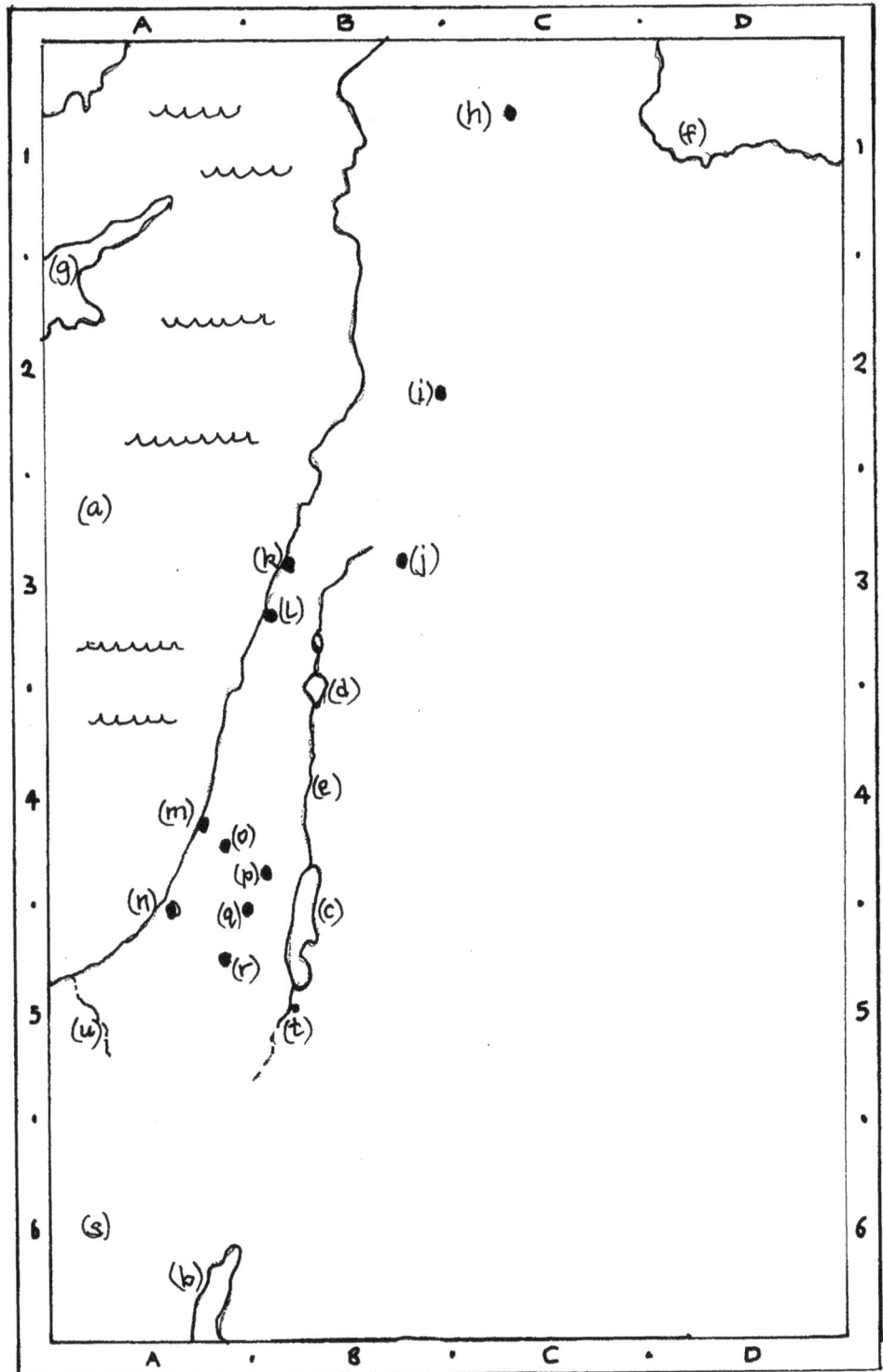

Where on Earth? Part 4: (cont'd)

Now match the place names in the column with the letters on the map.

Place Names

Aleppo

Beersheba

Damascus

Euphrates River

Gaza

Gezer

Gulf of Aqaba

Hebron

Jerusalem

Joppa

Jordan River

Kadesh

Kittim

(= *Cyprus*)

Salt Sea

(=*Dead Sea*)

Sea of Kinnereth

(= *Sea of Galilee*)

Sidon

Sinai

Tamar

The Great Sea

Tyre

Wadi of Egypt

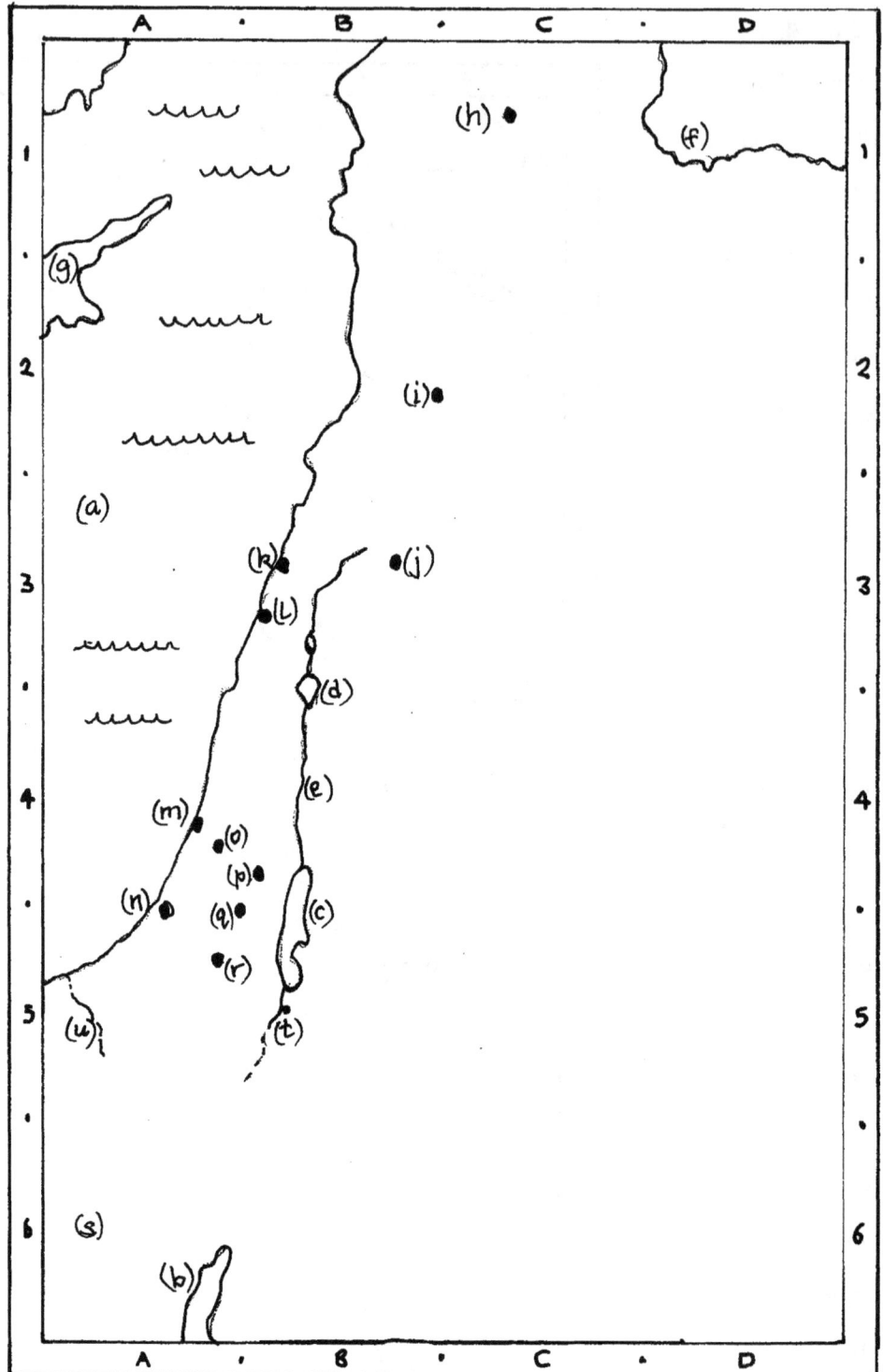

Score: . . ./ 21

Recall and Revisit

1 Name as many of the 11 faithful Apostles as you can:

_ _ _ _ _ _ _ _   _ _ _ _ _ _ _ _

_ _ _ _ _ _ _ _   _ _ _ _ _ _ _ _

_ _ _ _ _ _ _ _   _ _ _ _ _ _ _ _

_ _ _ _ _ _ _ _   _ _ _ _ _ _ _ _

_ _ _ _ _ _ _ _   _ _ _ _ _ _ _ _

_ _ _ _ _ _ _ _

2 The 12ᵗʰ, who betrayed Jesus for 30 pieces of silver, was _ _ _ _ _ _ _ _

3 Who was chosen to take his place?

_ _ _ _ _ _ _ _

4 Complete with the apostle's name.

_ _ _ _ _ _ _ _, the Evangelist

_ _ _ _ _ _ _ _, Rock

_ _ _ _ _ _ _ _, the Zealot or Zealous

_ _ _ _ _ _ _ _, Patron of Impossible Cases

_ _ _ _ _ _ _ _, tax collector, Alphaeus' son

Called '_ _ _ _ _ the Just' or 'St _ _ _ _ the Less'

Doubting _ _ _ _ _ believed when he saw.

Both Apostles & brothers _ _ _ _ _ _ _ _

5 The apostles were men from which area? _ _ _ _ _ _ _ _ _ _

6 The 'Road to Damascus' convert to the faith was _ _ _ _ whose name changed to _ _ _ _ and who was commissioned to preach the Good News to the _ _ _ _ _ _ _.

7 List the 9 gifts of the Holy Spirit:

_ _ _ _ _ _ _ _ _   _ _ _ _ _ _ _ _ _

_ _ _ _ _ _ _ _ _   _ _ _ _ _ _ _ _ _

_ _ _ _ _ _ _ _ _   _ _ _ _ _ _ _ _ _

_ _ _ _ _ _ _ _ _   _ _ _ _ _ _ _ _ _

_ _ _ _ _ _ _ _

8 Which of the gifts did King Solomon choose? _ _ _ _ _ _ _ _

9 What signs of the presence of the Holy Spirit manifested when the Apostles (at Pentecost) were blessed with gifts of the Spirit?

_ _ _ _ _ _ _ _ _ _ _ _ _ _ _ _ _

_ _ _ _ _ _ _ _ _ _ _ _ _ _ _ _ _

_ _ _ _ _ _ _ _ _ _ _ _ _ _ _ _ _

_ _ _ _ _ _ _ _ _ _ _ _ _ _ _ _ _

_ _ _ _ _ _ _ _ _ _ _ _ _ _ _ _ _

ANSWERS TO Recall and Revisit

1 Name as many of the 11 faithful apostles as you can:

PETER	*JOHN*
JAMES	*ANDREW*
PHILIP	*THOMAS*
BARTHOLEMEW	*MATTHEW*
JAMES	*SIMON*

JUDE

2 The 12th, who betrayed Jesus for 30 pieces of silver, was *JUDAS ISCARIOT*

3 Who was chosen to take his place?

MATTHIAS

4 Complete with the apostle's name.

JOHN, the Evangelist

PETER, Rock

SIMON, the Zealot or Zealous

JUDE, Patron of Impossible Cases

MATTHEW, tax collector, Alphaeus' son

Called '*JOHN* the Just' or '*St JOHN the Less*'

Doubting *THOMAS* believed when he saw.

Both Apostles & brothers *JOHN the Evangelist & James* (*sons of Zebedee*)

The apostles were men from which area? *GALILEE*

5 The 'Road to Damascus' convert to the faith was *SAUL* whose name changed to *PAUL* and who was commissioned to preach the Good News to the *GENTILES*.

6 List the 9 gifts of the Holy Spirit:

(MESSAGE of) WISDOM,
(MESSAGE of) KNOWLEDGE,
FAITH, GIFT of HEALING,
GIFT OF MIRACULOUS POWER,
PROPHESY, DISTINGUISHING between SPIRITS,
SPEAKING in TONGUES.
INTERPRETING WHAT WAS SAID in TONGUES

7 Which of the gifts did King Solomon choose? *WISDOM*

8 What signs of the presence of the Holy Spirit manifested when the Apostles (at Pentecost) were blessed with gifts of the Spirit?

The sound of a mighty wind; appearance of 'cloven tongues' of fire; apostles touched by the 'tongues'; Apostles speaking in other tongues - the languages of those in the crowd gathered outside the house.
(Acts 2: 1 . . . .)

My Notes:

_____
_____
_____
_____
_____
_____
_____
_____
_____
_____
_____
_____
_____
_____

From the Wisdom of King Solomon – *Where there is no guidance, a nation falls.*

Hatred stirs up strife, but love covers all offences. It is better to be poor than a liar.

The simple believe everything, but the clever consider their steps.

Like vinegar to the teeth and smoke to the eyes, so are the lazy to their employers.

On the lips of one who has understanding wisdom is found.

Whoever heeds instruction is on the path to life, but one who rejects a rebuke goes astray.

It is senseless to give a pledge for surety to your neighbour.   Grandchildren are the crown of the aged.

Whoever walks with the wise becomes wise, but the companion of fools suffers harm.

Those who oppress the poor insult their Maker, but those who are kind to the needy honour Him.

My Notes:

_____

_____

_____

_____

_____

_____

_____

_____

_____

_____

_____

_____

From the Wisdom of King Solomon

Whoever corrects a scoffer, wins abuse.   A scoffer who is rebuked will only hate you.

A wise child makes a glad father, but a foolish child is a mother's grief.

Wealth brings many friends.   A friend loves at all times.   Buy truth but do not sell it.

Whoever walks in integrity walks securely but whoever follows the perverse will be found out.

A good name is more valuable than riches.   Doing wrong is like sport to a fool.

Whoever belittles another lacks sense, but an intelligent person remains silent.

Those who love their children are diligent to discipline them.   A soft answer turns away wrath.

Pride goes before destruction and a haughty spirit before a fall.

Bibliography

VERSIONS OF THE BIBLES:

The Jerusalem Bible - Reader's Edition

Darton, Longman & Todd OR
Double Day & Company, New York

The NIV Study Bible - New International Version

Zondervan Bible Publishers,
Grand Rapids, Michigan 49506, USA

The NRSV – New Revised Standard Version

Harper Collins Publishers
353 Sacramento Street,
San Francisco CA 94111-3653

The Ryrie Study Bible - King James Version

Moody Press, Chicago

LODI, E., 'Saints of the Roman Calendar'

The Fathers and Brothers of the Society of St. Paul,
2187 Victory Boulevard, Staten Island,
New York 10314-6603   2012

NORWICH, J.J., 'The Popes – A History'

Vintage Books, London 2012

About the Author

M.J.Caimbeul is a teacher who has taught every year level from 1 to 12, served as a principal for several years, then became an adviser in and writer (and editor) of curriculum support material for Science, Environmental Studies and strands of Agriculture for distribution to state schools.

She is forever grateful to her employer and to her profession for exciting challenges, unique opportunities, and the very many wonderful people she has had the pleasure of meeting everywhere.